STONE CHILD'S
M O T H E R

Peter –
Renaissance man 😊

Virginia

STONE CHILD'S MOTHER

A Jungian Narrative Reflection on the Mother Archetype

VIRGINIA NEMETZ

iUniverse, Inc.
Bloomington

Stone Child's Mother
A Jungian Narrative Reflection on the Mother Archetype

iUniverse books may be ordered through booksellers or by contacting:

iUniverse
1663 Liberty Drive
Bloomington, IN 47403
www.iuniverse.com
1-800-Authors (1-800-288-4677)

Because of the dynamic nature of the Internet, any web addresses or links contained in this book may have changed since publication and may no longer be valid. The views expressed in this work are solely those of the author and do not necessarily reflect the ssviews of the publisher, and the publisher hereby disclaims any responsibility for them.

Any people depicted in stock imagery provided by Thinkstock are models, and such images are being used for illustrative purposes only.
Certain stock imagery © Thinkstock.

Cover Design: P. Moller / Egg Press Co.

ISBN: 978-1-4620-7294-1 (sc)
ISBN: 978-1-4620-7296-5 (hc)
ISBN: 978-1-4620-7298-9 (ebk)

Library of Congress Control Number: 2011962704

Printed in the United States of America

iUniverse rev. date: 01/12/2012

For my Mother

ADVANCE PRAISE FOR STONE CHILD'S MOTHER

"In this beautifully crafted and wise book, Nemetz humbly and honestly, through the vehicle of the mother archetype, shares her quest for wholeness, and, in the process, will certainly help other women understand their personal spiritual journey."
—Nellie A. Rodomsky, MD, PhD, author of Lost Voices: Women, Chronic Pain, and Abuse

". . . beautifully written … language rich in emotional metaphor . . . as the author guides us through lush pathways of archetypal imagery, we uncover a journey of spiritual struggle, awakening, and consciousness. Her graceful blending of art, literature, poetry, and Jungian psychology creates a narrative that at once nurtures the soul and stimulates our intellectual curiosity."
—Janet Gold, PhD, author of Clementina

"Is there anything new to say about mothers? Yes, there is, and Virginia Nemetz has shared it with the readers of her remarkable book, Stone Child's Mother. Grounded in Jungian psychology, Virginia introduces us to the loving mother, the nurturing mother, the transformational mother, the dark mother, and several other facets of the mother archetype. Indeed, there is a mother for all seasons, and Virginia has written a book for all the right reasons."
—Stanley Krippner, PhD, coauthor of Personal Mythology

"Virginia Nemetz has the unusual gift to write about the mother archetype in its personal and symbolic aspect. Her own lifelong quest is beautifully interwoven with the universal background. Fluently written, her book will capture the longing of so many who yearn for union with the female core of the journey in tune with the ever changing and life-giving mother energy in its dark, light and spiritual aspects, which guide the lives of women. This beautiful book touched me deeply. It is genuine and shares Virginia's journey in a generous way."

—Kathrin Asper, PhD, author of The Inner Child in Dreams and The Abandoned Child Within: On Losing and Regaining Self-Worth

CONTENTS

INTRODUCTION

This book is about mothers. It begins with the Buddhist tenet that we have all been mothers at one time. It is autobiographical because I am the stone child in the title. I have been a mother and I have struggled in my relationship with my own mother. Most likely I will continue to do so until I die. Struggles are good endeavors. From our struggles to understand we learn.

There is an American Native myth that goes like this. In the beginning, Sky Father and Earth Mother united. From their union Stone Child was created. When Stone Child was born into this world, she looked around and realized it was up to her to transform herself. This is where my story begins. This effort at transformation has been a life long task. I believe we are all capable of transformation and that we are all created for this experience. Because I have gained so much from my efforts, I hope that everyone who reads this book will feel motivated to undertake their own personal quest.

To sculpt a refined form out of stone takes patience. A piece of unconscious and amorphous stone that is chiseled into awareness and form goes through a re-creation. It is a process that we cultivate to find our purpose in life and to acknowledge who we are.

As a psychologist with a specialty in analytical psychology, also known as Jungian analysis, my perspective has grown out of work with the writings of C. G. Jung. Prior to my study of Jung's work, I became acquainted with Swami Sivananda Radha and her work with light and the practice of kundalini yoga. To my surprise Jung had also been influenced by the study of kundalini yoga. So I took my understanding of archetypes and their function from Jung's writing and from my study at the C. G. Jung Institute in Kusnacht, Switzerland. At the same time I realized the importance of kundalini yoga, as explained by Swami Radha, as an applied understanding of archetypes and their manifestations in daily life. Since archetypes are soul imprints, the mother archetype is the first archetype we encounter, even before our birth some would insist. Today, the word soul seems to be interchangeable with self. To understand the mother archetype, therefore, is to begin to understand one's self.

The importance of Jung's work in the field of psychoanalysis is far reaching. It can be said that he was the first psychologist to acknowledge the spirit. Not only did he acknowledge the importance of the spirit, he insisted that the basis of most neurotic behavior had its origin in the restless and unattended spirit or soul. In other words, the source of most sorrow and dis-ease in this world had to do with a distraught spirit. In my practice I am confronted with this phenomenon on a daily basis. Once the domain of Mother Church, the soul has been left behind in our fast paced world.

I have come to value this soul work because it is so important to our welfare. I see great changes in those who acknowledge their spiritual nature. I have come to this realization not only through observing the lives of my clients as they unfold and flower but also through my own spiritual practices and experiences. In a practical sense I recognize archetypes in the dreams, fantasies, stories and personal myths of those around me. Everyone has a story. Every life is unique. Therefore, our spirits manifest differently in reaction to each experience. Transformation is possible in every one of us.

Since most readers will never have been in analysis, my approach to the mother archetype will appear novel to some and cumbersome to others. Before I go any further into my own story, I must remind those of you who are sitting quietly and reading my book that the process of awareness is not acquired in a chronological manner. Neither is the process logical. It is random and, in this case, mine. As you read, be patient. Your own moments of insight may eventually occur to you or they may not. Some of my insights are shared and common; others are individual. My meandering process is my own. The subject of mother is a global and complex one. Despite my tendency to wander or to halt to catch my breath, I do realize it is my responsibility to communicate my insights as clearly as possible.

In other words, I have done what any analysand is expected to do in the course of their own psychoanalytical treatment. The process is rich and fulfilling and gives meaning to our efforts to find purpose in life.

If some of these reflections seem aimless, that is because they reflect the course of my own process. Mine has not been a straight path.

This book is divided into ten chapters. Each chapter contains psychological, artistic and spiritual concerns. Through the vehicle of the mother archetype I have attempted to explore and to integrate these concerns in my quest for wholeness. To that end I have encapsulated aspects of the psyche, known as the center of the soul, to hold together my own story. This story is augmented by my own dreams as well as by relevant dreams from the lives of clients.

I decided to write this book to share milestones on my own journey. So I begin by asking, "What is an archetype?" Jung, like Plato, defined an archetype as that soul imprint with which we are born. Imagine a mother duck being followed by her ducklings as they swim along the shore. In fact, archetypes are also our inherited tendencies, which form the collective treasure of wisdom that resides in the unconscious. There are other archetypes besides mother: father, marriage, sacred animals and shapes, the child, kings and queens and even death, for instance. Therefore, all the big important events in our life reveal archetypes of figures and events. Archetypes are the stuff of myths and fairy tales, dreams and fantasy. They also make themselves clear in our prayers and spiritual practices. The hero archetype has thrilled us in poetry, literature and legend. The mother archetype is monumental; she is arguably the first archetype we will encounter. Today's mothers bear the same joys and sorrows they have borne since ancient times. New mothers, old mothers, and even motherless children: this book helps to define her parameters. Because the mother archetype has played an integral role in my life and in the lives of my clients, I learn something new every day about her importance.

I begin this exploration of the mother archetype with birth. Chapter one is an introduction to mother in an archetypal context. Our life task is often presented to us with our entry into the world. Whether mother is or is not emotionally available to the child, she is, nevertheless, the vehicle of a new soul's journey. Chapters two and three not only explore the wide expanse of this archetype in greater depth, they do so by describing the helpmates we find on our way: grandmothers, substitute mothers and our growing awareness of the influence of mother in daily life. Chapters four and five magnify our understanding of the widespread contracts we have created to stay attached to this archetype. The church is a comfortable example. The discussion of any archetype would not be complete without an exploration of its other or dark connotations, so chapter six briefly explains the power of the negative mother complex that can manifest from this all consuming aspect of the archetype.

Chapters seven through ten address more diffuse connections of the archetype: dreams, energies, personal transformations and redemption or reconciliation of the archetype through my own reconnection to mother; these focus mostly on my own experience, for I cannot claim to know how the process will manifest in the lives of others. I do know I have observed the most astonishing and unexpected transformations in clients. Trust in a process that is orchestrated by an archetypal soul-awareness is an adventure, one whose outcome I could have never planned beforehand.

My own journey has included the practice of yoga, reaching out through writing poetry, the wisdom I have gained in my work with native elders, my own inspirations and those I have borrowed from the greatest literature. My beloved analyst Dr. Ian Baker guided my studies at the C. G. Jung Institute. The friendships I have sustained over decades of work at this process have contributed greatly to my persistence on this path. I hope my shared experience will help readers to be inspired similarly to step foot on this most rewarding psycho-spiritual quest. Though it may take a lifetime, the time will pass whether one is on the path or not. I recommend the path.

ACKNOWLEDGEMENTS

This work combines Jungian theory, first-hand experience, yogic and aboriginal wisdom. My long-time friendship with Swami Sivananda Radha taught me about my soul's quest. She once noted that my knowledge of women was whole and profoundly central to my psyche. My friendship with Cheryl Makokis whose Cree family name is Stone Child, introduced me to Native wisdom. Through her my compassion for other women as mothers has emerged. My decades of friendship with Kathleen Dunne helped me to mother my own daughter and to grow and blossom as a woman through my own self-acceptance.

Many others deserve recognition for their belief in my ability to share my experiences, that others might find them beneficial. Craig Stephenson read my first draft. How many people could be trusted with such a tender task? Christel Johanssen and my sister Janet read the second draft with intelligent and generous natures. Then, Brad, my beloved husband, stepped in to encourage another draft. He did it with sensitivity and love.

To my clients, whose lives and dreams are camouflaged but clear, I owe much on the path to my own understanding. Thank you for sharing, for your honesty and for your willingness to embark on the long journey that is self-realization.

To Nancy Read and Denise Guichon, thank you for listening and for editing; to Sister Lisbeth Simmons, thank you for praying; to Martin Sutcliffe, thank you for asking questions to add clarity; to my daughter Clea Huston, thank you for being so loyal and big-hearted. You have encouraged me to find my own voice. Remember the many hours that you insisted we work together to sculpt the Black Madonna? Thank you for being who you are.

If I have missed anyone, you can be sure you are in my heart. Thank you all.

At the time of Creation Sky Father united with Earth Mother and from their union was born Stone Child. At birth Stone Child knew instinctively that it would be her task to transform herself. To this end she stepped on the Spirit Path.

American Native Creation Myth

1

Mother Archetype:
Birth Trauma &
Rebirth

In the beginning are the womb and our first encounter with mother. She is the whole world. We become imprinted in her soul, and she is imprinted in our body. The life she channels is a gift of creation and becomes our connection with that divine spark in our center. The encounter gives us our breath and soul, and then catapults us into the unknown. This heritage of mother is our experience of the archetype of mother and within her embrace is all of creation. It has been said that "To walk through life armored against all fear, peril and disaster, only two things are needed, two that go always together—the Grace of the Divine Mother and on your side an inner state made up of faith, sincerity and surrender."[1]

In a small cottage by the river behind Abeling's Cider Mill, what held my attention as I lay on my back, gazing up at the window, were the dust motes suspended above me while light particles played on the air just out of reach. These fragments of light delighted me, reached inside me, held and nourished me. I opened my hand to grasp what I saw, and for a moment warmth soaked my palm, then disappeared. Envisioned before I could walk, light appears to have been my birth gift, and I know it is a gift each of us was given as our birthright.

The fact that my own mother was not one of my first memories only meant that I needed to struggle to remember and understand what I already knew. The fact that my first memory was that of light reaches out to hold me and sustain my life's efforts. Like Keats, whose "Ode to Psyche" was seen in descending Michaelangelic shafts of light, I, too, am inspired. "I see, and sing, by my own eyes inspired,"[2] wrote Keats. My first memory, never forgotten, recalled in unforeseen moments, surely points to the psyche's powerful reach and luminous hold. If the psyche is that wonder that accompanies the soul, the wonder that descends on a light beam or soaks into a child's palm, then it may be assumed that the psyche has been with us from the beginning. She is the wind and the heart of a bear. She is a friend without whom life is incomplete. Often, in order to find her, we begin our search for the soul.

There are quiet moments when, like a bit of dust descending in the room, I drift in and out of days with no thought to time being allotted in small mote-like portions or in fluffs of dust or in the grains of sandy eternity. How do I remind myself of time passing me by, when there is a sink to clean, garbage to take out, or dishes to remove from the dishwasher? My mind is a child of illusion whose keystone of comfort is memory. Whether or not the past is redeemable through memory remains unknown. That is, can I resurrect that feeling of warmth and security that was mother's shelter, recall the touch and warmth of light on baby skin, feel the gentle water of the womb? I am told that my time in utero did not go so well for me. Mother fell down a flight of stairs and I was spun around, legs twisted and hips squeezed. Birth was not an easy time for either of us. Not that it mattered that my birth was traumatic or that my arrival was a hardship to be endured. Certainly, I was healthy and strong and happy to be here.

In the beginning there is birth. Otto Rank, an early pioneer in the field of psychoanalysis, spoke of birth as a trauma. It is essentially the trauma of separation from mother. Subsequently, death becomes a reuniting with mother and her dark warm womb. In the beginning mothers dominated cultural traditions, and a mother's rights were considered an essential aspect of consciousness. J. J. Bachofen was a Swiss thinker who emphasized the importance of mother understanding. He was concerned with matriarchy before it was taken over by the masculine influence that put a curse on women's organs and tried to repress or control those organs. Obviously, the birth process refers to the primary and most enviable act: creation. In an effort to camouflage this envy, men have subjected women to mutilations, have covered them from head to toe, have kept them behind walls and have protected them from the deleterious effects of education. According to Freud, a young boy's unconscious desire for the ability to give birth is sublimated quickly in our cultural era to the desire to control those who actually give birth. Women are beaten, humiliated and kept at home, all in a more or less unconscious desire to obliterate the power of creation. As birth and death are inextricably connected, so are creation and destruction. One can quickly turn to the other.

Whether they realize it or not, mothers are powerful. In a compendium of goddesses representing mother, one of the earliest is the Sphinx. In ancient Phoenician, Egyptian and Peruvian myths, she stands guard inscrutably over coffins and graves. Known as the goddess of death, she is also a receptacle of birth; for the human head is what she births. As a powerful woman, she dictates that men be excluded from the act of mourning.

Death is a return to the womb, and the wailing that accompanies the mourning ritual is a call to this return to the earth. "Indeed, the ancients recognized in this taking back of the dead, the highest expression of mother love which keeps faith with her offspring of the moment, when it stands there abandoned by all."[3] Thus, visitors to Egypt still stand in awe before her magisterial presence as she presides over the pyramids, the ancient burial grounds of an ancient culture.

Though my first memories had nothing to do with mother, this book has everything to do with mother: my own, myself as mother, spiritual mothers, Divine Mother, ordinary mothers and the archetype of mother. My path would soon involve a search for her.

Plato was the earliest known philosopher to use the word archetype. As an image, the archetype is the imprint of the Divine as it touches the soul. It manifests in the form of dreams, visions and mythical awareness, all of which derive from the domain of the unconscious. In the *Phaedo,* Plato remarked that "if it is true that we acquired our knowledge before our birth, and lost it at the moment of birth but afterward, by the exercise of our senses upon sensible objects, recovered the knowledge which we had once before, I suppose that what we call learning will be the recovery of our own knowledge . . ."[4]

When Plato referred to the archetype, he was referring to the light and the idea of the light's image: the Light of all Light. Today Plato's insights are referred to as religious philosophy, and the light he spoke of might be described through images of Christ instead, or the Light of Heaven. Plato's thoughts have been categorized, classified and divided by reason and logic while the psyche has been relegated to the field of alternative studies.

Gestation, birth, birth trauma and severance from the mother vessel: all these states of development rely on mother. Without her we would not be here. It is a big subject, never more so than now in the twenty-first century, when motherhood has become an arduous task for some, a distant phenomenon for others. After all, so much can go wrong; humans are not perfect; therefore, mothers are apt to be blamed for the messy misunderstandings that accompany the growth process. Blame, it would seem, comes with the territory.

When my mother was eighty, she came to visit. It was a time spent in slow motion. Time is a gift, I told myself, not a trial but an opportunity to go into slow motion in an imitation of my mother's age and pace, an opportunity to experience her perception of time. No visit ever happens twice. Nothing is more sacred than this moment. I bought lots of yarn and began a knitting project to fill in the long silences, to bring together the strands of my life and to untie the intermittent pain I felt as heaviness descended. My mother had never held me tenderly or said, "I love you". She never got that quality of delight in her voice, when she spoke of me or to me. She was not about to change at eighty.

On the first night of her visit I had a dream. In the dream I take my mother for a visit to Yasodhara Ashram. On our first day we walk together up the steps that lead to the backdoor of the ashram bookstore. It is winter, snowy and cold, but the bookstore is warm inside. The heat comes from a little wood-burning stove in the middle of the store. Swami Brahmananda sits at the book order desk, and I introduce him to my mother.

Most psychologists would interpret this dream as compensatory, meant to fulfill us in areas that are lacking in our real lives. Longing for mother is expressed in the desire to return to a warm and comfortable room that is filled with the dreamer's favorite things, in this case books. The books are mostly spiritual and can be ordered right there. The keeper of the store is a curious and holy monk with the name Brahmananda or bliss of Brahma or, more accurately, the bliss of creation. Obviously, I still wish for a joyous birth and for acceptance by mother, for no one escapes the trauma of birth. There is always a satisfaction in showing something to mother. Every child wants to exclaim, "Look Ma, no hands." It is evidence of mastery of a task and is often the foundation of confidence and competence.

To regard the dream as mere compensation, however, would be too simple. This dream is really about the act of creation. The warmth of the stove is the warmth and comfort of centeredness and love. Love of knowledge is what I wish to share with mother. Swami Brahmananda is my friend in reality, and his name evokes creativity. The fire still burns warmly at the center of my world. It remains for me to sublimate into personal fulfillment this constant yearning for mother's acceptance

This dream of mother and the dream's interpretation brings to mind other aspects of mother: birth and womb. Here in the bookstore, it is cozy and warm and filled with beloved knowledge, collected-wisdom-filled shelves and an access to more knowledge at Brahmananda's desk. The bookstore is a living structure in the sense that it is a place alive with dreams. It is similar to the image of a house, a house being a symbol for the self. In its womb-like container, the house shelters the person, providing comfort and an inner relationship to that which surrounds it. The work of archeologist Ernst Fuhrmann reveals that man often placed a living-human-child sacrifice "into the foundation of a new house".[5] Thus, new life was expected to flourish in the position of a fetus in this womb-like home. The gods were placated, and so the occupants were safe and protected. Such obvious symbolic action comes directly from our fear of being suddenly on our own without a mother's secure warmth.

Mother's visit unbalanced me. It is an embarrassment to admit a need for acceptance at my age. It seems that this constant craving has been with me since birth. Many of my life lessons have been about acceptance—so many, in fact, that I finally became aware of a pattern. It is as if the universe gives me reminders whenever I fail to accept myself. "Here," it says, "have another try."

Most people spend an entire lifetime trying to undo birth trauma, denying separation from mother and gaining an identity separate from mother. In biblical times there was a flood that nearly eliminated humans from the earth. In this act of nature, earth expelled her children, and they were suddenly on their own. This flood is an example of a universal reaction to birth trauma. Noah's response was to build a boat or a mother vessel in which he placed all the animals in pairs, a formula for survival, a way to go back to the womb and to gestate some more.

We refer to the phrase 'back to nature' as a connection to the forest or to the sea or to Mother Nature. We destroy the earth's resources as we bathe in the sun's warmth, swim in an embryonic sea, climb mountains that resemble her breasts or rest in mountain caves resembling her womb. We manufacture beautiful and warm clothing to re-experience being back inside of mother, away from the cold exposure of birth. Rapists try to return to the womb, and singers cry out their emotions in order to breathe away the tension and anxiety of separation from her. The vast majority still blames mother for its problems, beginning with the pain and fear of the loss of the embryonic caul. This includes the umbilical cord that is discarded in the hospital at birth.

This quest for mother is as ancient as motherhood, and each one of us is subject to these yearnings in one form or another. Sometimes we refer to such yearning as craving, a desire that may be fulfilled only rarely. We forget that our mothers had their own mothers and they, in turn, had theirs. Meanwhile, pain survives time and the grave. One need only ask an addict, who is quite aware of the intense pain of longing, what it feels like never to be satisfied.

When we are conceived, our earliest relationship is the environment in mother's womb. A pre-natal connection is there between mother and child. We turn from side to side and swim in the Edenic water. We hear through the bones in our skull her voice and the beat of her heart. Our relationship is physiological. Comfort, warmth and food create wellbeing, and all that is asked of us is to grow. Our wisdom is cellular. The great abortion debate centers on this wisdom, or more specifically, on the soul and our definition of when soul enters the body. Some say the soul *is* the body, that they are one and the same; others believe that until the embryo is able to survive on its own it is not a human soul. The Eastern belief is that until the first breath has been taken in this atmosphere there is no soul; for soul is the breath. There is so much controversy. Some believe that each child chooses its own parents before conception. That belief is based on the choice of tasks or experiences we need to deal with in this lifetime. Perhaps it is true, then, that we choose our mothers. Perhaps it is also true that we repeat our birth many times in order to learn to detach ourselves from mother.

Several years ago my mother admitted to me that she had always been envious of her children, all of them, without exception. She hopes to change her attitude but envious feelings still afflict her.

Envy is fundamental to psychoanalytic therapy. To overcome envy is to acquire a mastery over the trauma of birth. Child psychoanalyst, Melanie Klein furthers our understanding of this grievous evil so prevalent in the world today. It is the root of much violence. In her book *Envy* Klein refers to the Old Testament and its exposure of this universal problem. Also, envy is one of the seven deadly sins listed in the Catholic catechism as a flaw of human nature. Klein's description of envy, however, exposes its opposite, which is great love and generosity. Her enlargement of the problem shows us the lessons that can be learned from envy and its dark projections. Light added to envy creates love and understanding. Giving is a counteraction to envy's negative and soul-destroying behavior. Giving reverses the urge to be needy, often referred to as greedy. Envy, transformed to giving, becomes a spiritual practice and is not confined to the world of material possessions. When magnified envy includes covetous thoughts. It involves our behavior toward the success, sympathetic joy, happiness and goodness of another's actions. Birth is mother's first act of giving.

No wonder birth is traumatic; it is the expulsion from Eden. Now begins the real journey. The trauma of birth becomes synonymous with a chance to become conscious and to leave behind the suffering to which we are all subjected. Envy, for instance, must be left behind as we are expelled from Eden. The journey of the hero or heroine starts with mother acceptance. Every individual seeks a strong armor and eventually a redeeming love, as a reward for courage and heroic deeds.

When my mother admitted her state of envy, I had to admire her honesty. A mother's journey is oceanic. It is an hormonal, emotional and heroic experience. It occurs when a girl leaves the garden of childhood to embrace womanhood. As part of her experience her body changes and there are moments when she no longer recognizes her old self. Part of my mother's envy may have been a wish to return to an easier way of life. My birth cancelled that option.

As for me, I ask myself who would be interested in the close study of an ordinary woman, a mother whose claim to fame is absent. How wonderful it would be, I imagine, to site important works of art or acts of human kindness to sum up a life of productivity and renown. Instead, my mind wanders. I wonder what my ninety-year-old mother is thinking, as she sits in her recliner in the living room most of the day; quiet, reflective, a bit sad it seems to me. Now that I have reached a crossroad in my life, I find a need to weave, as accurately and as sincerely as possible, the events of my life, to gather unforgotten images, to construct a mural that depicts some awareness of where I have been and how I arrived here. In the end, I do this in the belief that one life lived to its fullest is worth the struggle. As I seek a unifying theme or image, a numinous mother emerges. She rocks by my side in her recliner. She is my own image, my mother, all the mothers on earth; and she is backlit with an eternal glow. Love takes only a moment; hatred and indifference that develop from envy or from any other derived form of birth trauma may consume and destroy a lifetime.

The other side of birth trauma is the trauma of birth for mother. In old myths and fairy tales there is no direct mention of trauma. Women gave birth in fields, got up and continued their day's work with baby strapped on their backs. Only occasionally is there mention of a vengeful goddess or a despairing mother who throws her child from a bridge. Most women were simply grateful for having survived the birth.

Most women who give birth experience some form of post-partum blues and a certain percentage of these will experience depression. Occasionally, there is the tragedy of psychosis. Most of this experience is physical and hormone related, though hormones are also related to mother's pre and post birth state of mind. Loss comes up suddenly and unexpectedly. How could the arrival of such a precious little person be accompanied by anxiety, loss of sleep, fear of inadequacy, resentment and the realization that life will never again be the same? Trauma seeps down to a physiological level, cellular and alive.

In a child's world the typical reaction to loss that threatens security is depicted most often through fairy tales and hero myths that symbolize a need for emotional compensation. After all, the hero or heroine in the fairy tale is usually a child. Take the popular book by Maurice Sendak that recently became a fine movie produced by Tom Hanks. *Where the Wild Things Are* is the story of one little boy who faces the loss of his father and a separation from his mother. All in one night of rebellion in his dreams, he voyages to a land of scary monsters. He tames the monsters, only to discover that what they needed was love. His is a journey of the young hero, one that many children in modern times must undertake. Max's dilemma is his parents' divorce. His father has left the home and his mother is dating other men. Max has lost the security of his birthright and he is terribly angry and hurt. However, he discovers all the same problems among the big monsters: they cry, they hurt one another, they are not heard and they are sometimes mean and thoughtless.

Fairy tales and myths express essential human conditions such as trauma. In fairy tales mothers swallow their children, for example, or wean them by burning their lips. Such was the case of Achilles. The birth of a child is a stark reminder to mother of the essential human condition told to us in the Bible, that in pain shall children be brought forth. This was one of the original curses or traumas visited on mankind. It is a further reminder of death, for "everyone born sinks back again into the womb from which he or she once came into the realm of light . . . Everywhere woman appears as bearer of the law of death . . . capable of the deepest sympathy but also of the greatest severity."[6] The cycle of life is reflected in birth and death, creation and destruction, all of which are aspects of mother expressed in fairytales and myth.

The first and most universal symbol of mother and birth is the egg. Watch a chick being born. Whether it is head or feet first, the nourishment, once part of the egg, has gone to feed the embryo. What mother has laid and sat on is consumed by a new life. Beyond warmth, a few directions and food, mother is superfluous after the hatching of the chicken child.

In the human mother's world there can be hurt and resentment, expectations of idyllic care and loving by a husband, thoughts being turned up side down in hormonal upheaval, and the realization that life, as she knew it, will forever live in abeyance to this new life, this little stranger who demands love and constant attention. It is a great shock.

Recently, I conducted an information workshop on post-partum depression at a reservation of First Nation people. The mothers in the group were quite pregnant, and some of them had experienced a bluesy depression after previous pregnancies. Generally speaking, however, these women experienced less of this condition than the general population. Yet, in reality, native women fit the high-risk profile, in that many have been traumatized themselves. Perplexed, I asked the women if they might know the reason for their more positive outlook. Immediately, one woman responded, "Because we consider babies to be a blessing in comparison to non-native women." Perhaps this is true, maybe not. Do we consider our babies to be a blessing or are they an inconvenience to women who must go back to work as soon as their pregnancy leaves are up? A blessing? How many children do I see who are not blessings and never will be considered blessed? In fact, how many mothers are afraid of their children? These more negative thoughts can produce post-partum depression.

I look back at my dream of my mother and the bookstore. Brahamananda was there, and, too, was the warmth of the stove in the middle of the room. Brahma is the wonderful Hindu dual god of creation. As such, he is also a she or the goddess of creation. Between Brahma and his other half, reality and non-reality, what is and what is not, motion and stillness, unite. When Brahma appears, sacrifice is inevitable in order that there be transformation of the soul from its duality to a single and centered soul of transcendence. Mother-sacrifice must be attended by each of us. Separation from mother is inevitable. In that bookstore surrounded by knowledge, I knew what I had to do. I had to grow up, stop blaming, start to accept that this was my karma, my fate, and it was my responsibility to do something about it. If I had been a man, this task might have seemed more obvious and certainly a necessity. Being a woman, it was not so obvious to me how I might go about this task of separation from mother. The task would involve a fine discrimination or clarification of my own personality and its mother-defying image that, at this stage, resembled a formless mass. Thus I began to nibble on the golden egg that had enclosed me during gestation. I began to use what mother had provided for me to separate from her.

In the Hindu tradition initiates of holy rites are the pupils of the sacred Brahma. Metaphorically, they must stay within the womb of their teacher for three days, in a state of hypnosis. "The teacher who initiates the pupil makes of him an embryo in his inmost parts. Three nights he carries him in the womb. Then he brings forth him who comes to see the Gods."[7] This action constitutes what is certainly a holy sacrifice.

The position for entering the womb is known as 'uttana' in yoga asanas or postures, and is synonymous with the position of an embryo. It is also the position taken by traumatized catatonics. This pose symbolizes a desire to return to the uterus. There, the sounds of creation echo in the embryo's ear and the "milk of life" is actually remnants of dust from the stars or the Milky Way. The vital heat that exists there is the perfect temperature and nearby is mother's heart. Her heart is likened to the center of the wheel of life. The spokes of the wheel revolve while the hub remains motionless in a state of bliss. Thus, the embryo in utero resembles the hub of an enviable state of bliss.

When Mother tumbled down the stairs with me inside, I knew something was wrong. I sensed it was a prelude to what was to come, that is, my arduous birth. The feel of falling and of not being caught created in me a fear of heights. I was born with a jolt.

Here is a poignant quote from the Kleine Midraschim in the *Buch von der Schopfung des Kindes*. When the unborn child is shown dawn and sunset, that is heaven and hell, it then is shown where it will live and die on earth. After a brief glimpse at its future, the Angel leads it back again into the body of its mother, and the Holy One, praise be to him, makes doors and bolts for it. And the Holy One, praise be to him, says to it, 'As far as this shalt thou come and no further' . . . . 'Against your will have you been formed in your mother's womb, *and against your Will shall you be born to go out into the world.*' Immediately the Child weeps. And why does it weep? Just because of that world in which it was and which it now leaves. And as it goes out, the Angel strikes it under its nose and blots out the light over its head. He brings it out against its will and it forgets everything which it has seen. And as it comes out it weeps."[8]

Of course, the symbolic evildoer in this scenario is the mother who pushes the child into the world and out of paradise.

This expulsion from the womb brings us to the mythical and mystic rebirth mysteries in which the little embryo that is sacrificed is promised a day of return to the womb, to the place where nourishment is abundant and the worshiper becomes a god herself. The longing, constant and persistent, often felt throughout a lifetime, can be traced to this, the first and most primal of experiences, birth from a mother.[9]

As to my own mother, there has always existed an animosity, an underlying anger that, as a child, I could never comprehend, a begrudging acceptance of my very existence. Throughout the years I have tried to get her attention, even to buy her love. A decade ago she asked me to forgive her the hurt she had caused me. She felt guilt and sorrow for the way she had ignored, dismissed and rejected me. My first reaction was indignation. I found forgiveness to be impossible. Was I supposed to turn the other cheek on decades of dysfunctional poison? I was not that evolved spiritually. It would take me years, if ever, to overlook all that love that she could not give me.

What were my expectations? During my mother's visit, when I bought all that wool to knit, my great plan was to take her to the very ashram of my dreams, to the warm bookstore. My plan was for us to drive there together and my hope was that Mother would come to understand me, and a part of my life that I cherished. In my fantasies our relationship, consequently, would change to a warm and secure one, safe from indifference. The day I was making those plans, Mother overheard me on the phone, telling a friend how much I looked forward to this trip. Just after I put the phone down, she announced suddenly that she had changed her mind and no longer wished to visit an ashram.

From this encounter I had the feeling that my inherited task is to love myself and, thereby, witness and praise creation. This insight has been followed by many other revelations. As with any realization, a door opens. Several days after mother's visit, she phoned to chat. She has had a wonderful visit, she says, and ends the conversation saying, "I love you". When I least expect to hear those words, they are said aloud. Forgiveness hovers nearby. I realize in retrospect that, imperceptibly, healing may have taken place. What had taken place also was the realization that I had put aside my sorrow and disappointment and expectations. In the process of living, I had chosen to grow and to love and to give without the expectation that I would receive anything in return. I focus on my own tasks. Real mothers, mothers-in-law, aging mothers, motherless children, spiritual mothers, adopted mothers: all these demand attention. Creativity demands attention. Now, I write my poetry and a need to write crowds my every day. There cannot be too much creation.

Sometimes the process of creation begins with rebirth. Some of those first acts of creation took place in caves, in a womb-like atmosphere, protected from the sun and other harsh elements. Others began underground in the rites of Aesculepius, physician of the parched soul, who advocated a return to the underground chthonic world of dreams and creation. Aesculepius promoted the work of the spirit. Sublimation of the outward personality and the hermit-like interiority of spiritual practices such as austerity, withdrawal from the outer world with hard work, study and patience, were used to combat a deadening of the soul. Once a dream was dreamed in the primal environment of Aesculepius, the dream recipient had to go forth and obey the dream's message. The dry and brittle, overly masculine approach to the spirit, had to be overcome before inner strength was gained. This was my own epiphany, the moment when I realized that I needed to begin the long process of analysis, sort through the accumulation of diversions and false starts and be honest. Aesculepius was right.

Action is necessary. It is one thing to dream, another to follow the dream. In my practice I recognize this reaction time and again. Dreams are dreamed and then ignored. Clients often wait and hope for an easier answer, a clearer dream, until finally it comes in the form of a nightmare. Then great suffering and effort are at last undertaken to promote change. In Hindu myths of the Rig Veda the creator must incubate in her own womb, cook in her own heat, become pregnant from within. To do this one must go within and wait.

The process of self-realization is a form of rebirth. To choose to experience the anxiety of birth, and subsequently of rebirth, is an act of courage. The artist and the hero and even the analysand who choose to reconstruct and to understand a full life, value consciousness enough to subject themselves to profound inquiry. When exterior stressors intrude on life, there is a tendency to falter by holding up the shield that is a protective filter from that primal birth anxiety. These stressors may have a more violent impact on those who are in the process of becoming conscious. Health issues, death of a beloved, loss of a job and divorce are unavoidable daily stressors that combine and remind us of the past. Therefore, the hero, the artist, and the analysand spend years at their task, allowing for interruptions and slow downs. A long-term focus is necessary. It is a long and arduous process. To choose to experience the anxiety of a new birth takes persistence as well as courage, for it is a re-entry into the unknown. It takes a certain inner knowing ahead of time that this path is even possible and possibly productive. It is alchemical and can be likened to a prospector panning for gold.

Reuniting with the soul or the psyche necessarily involves a birth, a separation and, finally, a reunion or second birthing. Often what is not taken into consideration is the second trauma of a second birth, for birth is never a given. It is never to be taken for granted. The second or mystical birth must be done alone, even if it takes the outward form of marriage in the world between lover and beloved. Once the honeymoon is over and that intense and nearly psychotic union has taken place, there comes the next step that is a renewed search for the sense of self while in a state of emotional communion. In the case of rebirth the new being must stand in the light. It must be willing to bask in the presence of light, once self-mastery has begun to fertilize in the darkness. The chick, the baby, the newly wed and the artist blink at the intensity of the light, the often harsh exposure to criticism and abandonment, to the desiccating air, the hot breath, the extreme temperatures of emotion and the solitary task of the creator. It is an heroic leap from created creature to *creator mundi*. What this means is that once we are born, that is, created, the next step is to grow and partake of the life we have been given.

In Navajo myth the ancestors of Sky Father and Earth Mother mated atop a mountain to give birth to a stone. From their union a stone-child is born, and from her birth comes "the woman who rejuvenates or transforms herself".[10] The stone holds a vision that comes from a star. This, it would seem, was to be my path, to follow beams of light to their source within. I am a stone child.

Like the sculptor we must chip away at the stone to find the form within the stone. It is there and awaits our touch.

2

The Grandmothers:
Grannys, Shamans &
The Gift of the Prism

In place of mother what could be better than a good grandmother? She represents an enlargement of the mother archetype. She has lived in awe, which is the essence of worship. The passing of generations, like the continuation of new life, beckons to her. The prism that grandmother gave me scattered light. I learned that I could never hold on to that light; I was meant to share it.

In order to grow a child needs nurturance. It was fortunate for me that there was grandmother, who came to stay like a solid and comforting spirit. It was grandmother who left me her precious prism.

Beloved mythologist and teacher Joseph Campbell speaks of light in terms of reflected, projected and directed experience. The projected light is like light that has found its way through a prism; it is many colored and separated from its source into infinite facets. It goes through an experience, a crystal, for example, and finds itself divided and projected along angles and curves in which it had no intention of going. If emotion and reason go through the same process when they enter one person before going to another, the result is confusion.

The sage, Hui-neng steps out of his kitchen and waxes eloquent, as he describes the ephemeral experience of light and the body.

> The body is not the Bodhi Tree
> The mind is no mirror bright
> Since nothing is there
> On what should dust alight?[1]

On what do I alight? I remember the feel of peaceful saturation that penetrated the soft spot atop my head. Light falls on this paper and creates shadows, and I realize that light has created a kind of meaning in my life. Campbell's book *Myths of Light* reaches out from the shelf and I hand it to the cashier. Will these myths belie the fact that I have found comfort in the light?

I gather childhood photos, those few earliest ones that I can find. They sit for weeks in an alchemical pile on my desk until I can summon the courage to open the scrapbooks. Now what? On some level I am grateful to have started this project, for it gives purpose to the open floodgate of insights and questions of what I am to do with these overwhelming feelings that cry out to be collected and sorted. They shine a light on where I have been and help me to awaken to light within. On another level there is that ever-present wish to deny my past in a pretense of wellbeing. "Lighten up," I tell myself. "You are fortunate that in mid-life you underwent analysis. Many of these photos will have been discussed during analytical sessions." They are my personal myths. They explain the phenomenon of my life, which I wish to change to gold.

Take this image of me at age two. My sister is only a few months old and I think she is beautiful. She is supposed to be my friend, someone who will play with me any time now. It is very quiet in the room as sunlight slides between the blinds on the window. Janet is sleeping. I hear Mother calling me but I cannot answer or I will wake this tiny person who is lying directly beneath a beam of sunlight. In awe, I realize that the light has found her and is blessing her, its single ray aimed right at her, seeking her tiny form. I stand silently, waiting for the light to share its special gift with both of us. The bedroom door swings open abruptly.

The scenario that follows is a prelude to the years to come. Mother misconstrues my intentions. She is angry and tells me to get away from my sister. I start to cry and Janet wakens, startled. Grandmother tries to explain to Mother that there is no problem. No one considers the light, now scattered, as Mother crosses the room, and her shadow falls across the crib. Eventually, Janet quiets. We have missed out on the sunbeam experience. From this day on there is a label attached to my intentions. My mother attributes her suspicion to my behavior regarding my sister. I am two years old but apparently not innocent.

In his book *The Wind is My Mother,* Bear Heart relates the story of a four-year-old child who approaches his newborn sister in the peace and quiet of the nursery and whispers, "Tell me about God. I'm beginning to forget."[2] He knows his little sister still remembers, despite her distracting birth and the blankets that surround her.

The one who has not judged me is Grandmother. As time goes by, she becomes my stalwart champion, not by anything she says, but by her solid presence.

Nevertheless, my mother has set the myth in motion. I am to become the household scapegoat, bearing the blame for the mistakes of others. In her humble way, Grandmother understands what has happened. She speaks little English but she defends me and sacrifices one more credit in a household where she already lives on sufferance. She is father's mother, after all.

Since her death, my grandmother has appeared to me in a dream to assure me that she is still looking after me from the other side. As father's mother she was always there to offer wisdom, whenever my birth mother abandoned me emotionally. In death she continues to take on the work of my ally. She sits at the foot of my bed each night to let me know that she will never forget me. I am grateful for her protection, her guidance and her love.

My gratitude for my grandmother, who still watches over me, is profound; for in my mind my true mother is my father's mother who lived with us from the time I was two until I was nearly twelve. She was the one who cherished me, whom Mother disliked intensely, who did not speak English. Since I was not allowed to speak to her in Polish, grandmother spoke to me in Polish and I answered in English.

The archetype of the mother includes grandmothers, the light of creation—and its many projections. It is the first and greatest of the archetypes, both feared and revered. If an archetype can be defined as a primordial image, then the image of mother is our first image before we are born. We float inside mother, who has images and dreams of her own mother, and thus our psyche is structured cell by cell, organ by organ, with traces of wisdom and evolutionary patterns, regarding how we are to step onto our path of consciousness, our journey toward the light. The mother of our mother is powerful indeed. Shakespeare once said we are "a child of our grandmother."[3]

The subject of grandmothers leads directly to the larger subject of matriarchy and, of course, once again, projection. Anthropologist Robert Briffault's theory implies that those who are "preoccupied with the mother figure tend to envisage their deity as a mother, while those preoccupied with the father tend to postulate father deities."[4] I suspect I am preoccupied with finding mother.

This theory fits perfectly with a reverence for grandmothers, for their wisdom and their social direction. Grandmothers have been gathering in recent years, mostly throughout aboriginal cultures, but they have been called together spontaneously, unknown to one another, to perform certain rites of gratitude to Mother Earth. In doing so these women have wished to impart the importance of being handmaidens of Divine Mother. These grandmothers have instructed other women to pick up the pieces and to use nurturing skills in sacred service. Unless young women feel gratitude for nature and for creation, they cannot emerge from the destruction that will ensue, and each one will miss the purpose of her life, which is to grow in awe of creation.

Grandmothers wait in the wings for respect. They wait to be asked questions. Some of them do not seem to know much but others are wellsprings of wisdom and of gratitude. Their wisdom comes from experience and their gratitude comes from reflection. Through the power of their consciousness, they are holding the world in the light of love and prayer. Grandmothers transmit their wealth of knowledge, for they have been the weavers of collected wisdom. They have prepared animal skins for warmth and they have birthed their babies. They have held social groups together and have drawn the symbols that have preserved rites. These rites have been the containers for emotion. The grandmothers have documented whatever good and evil they have beheld.

Traditionally, women have been shamans, and their healing powers have been passed on from generation to generation. In order for a man to become a shaman, it was necessary that he become as much like a woman as possible.[5] At the time, the powers that were transmitted were referred to as grandmothers. When the patriarchy becomes overloaded with technologies, when their bleakness and destructive power have finished dazzling the world, let us hope that the grandmothers will still be here to mend the broken pieces, to weave them back together.

Today, the Sioux refer to the moon that presides over much of shamanic healing and magic as the old woman who never dies. The Maori people of New Zealand use a moon reference, too: Eternal One as grandmother. It would seem that the stature that grandmothers enjoyed as healers and wise ones occurred during a matriarchal era, a time that came before our present cycle of patriarchy.

In a patriarchal environment there is mention of a past that was controlled by the mother, who devoured men and her children in a dark feast of destruction. We have come to fear this type of grandmother or ancient mother. The last vestige of her influence in modern times is the dreaded mother-in-law who will not give up her reign.

Recently, grandmothers have been called into service to care for the children of failed marriages. In this way grandmothers have become reacquainted with the divine child archetype. I have seen these women in my office, confused, overburdened and saddened for the grandchildren of deprivation. More and more often grandmothers must step in to replace mothers who are working or who are simply incapable of dealing with modern demands and expectations of perfection. Grandmothers are not afraid to slow down, to sit, to watch and to allow creativity to take over from the technical bullying of automation.

My grandmother's face reappears. It is a funny face, full of wrinkles and smile lines around the eyes, eyes that twinkle. They really look at me. Her body appears next; it is short and rather round and soft. In the winters I hop quickly from my bed each morning and scramble to get into her bed, under the covers where I roll over again, down into a trough created by her body in the center of the old spring mattress. It is warm there and peaceful. I fall back to sleep, this time deeply, held securely by sweet dreams. In the summers I hug her a lot and am acquainted with her apron holes, which my small fingers have drilled through to her belly. There is no tension there, no rejection that I can feel. She sits on the sun porch or in the kitchen, quiet and non-judgmental, listening to disagreements and resentments. She has had decades of her own sorrow but is like Buddha, present in the moment, unshaken by the past or future.

She is a gardener. In the spring she tills and sows the earth; in the summer she weeds, each morning bent at the hips, bum in the air, carefully sorting the vegetables from the weeds. In the autumn she harvests and cans and cooks. In the winter she raids the root cellar to enjoy the fruits of her labor. In rhythm with the seasons and the cycles of life and death, she has seen plants and children come and go. One of her daughters died in childbirth at age sixteen. "Julia," I occasionally hear her murmur. It is not a loud murmur, but quiet in order to be sorrowful but still respectful of God's wrath. There is a time for everything under heaven. In the sphere of the grandmothers there are cycles and a rhythm of repetition of those intervals.

The archetypes of mother and grandmother intertwine. In its earliest conception the archetype or primordial image and what it represented was the "image of god that resided in humans".[6] In alchemical texts the image that is called forth by the archetype is that of light. Throughout the history of archetypal understanding there is that which has been transmitted to us from dreams and visions. A more elaborate form comes to us through mythic wisdom. The fact that this knowledge must come from the soul or from the collective wisdom of the unconscious is what makes it so mysterious. It reaches us from the psyche rather than from a more worldly orientation. Humankind has projected this inner knowing onto the outer and visible world of nature and onto religious rites and the symbolic expression of what is almost known, which includes the secrets of the sacred and the ecstasy of the beautiful or the ethereal. Thus, the archetype of the mother represents the first contact with the divine pool of creation and is accompanied by the special characteristics of all archetypes: it is numinous. To be numinous means to be aglow with drops of holy light. At the same time, it must be accompanied by the shadowy part of the unknown or the unconscious that is personal, warmed with the best of mother's heart and the food she ingests, both bread and tears. In the dark are the inherited memories of mother's mother that infuse the birth fluid. Vibrations of a greater knowledge of spiritual mysteries can infiltrate the uterus with darkness or with light.

In mother's womb we learn the paradox of suspension that concerns us only in so much as our waiting or floating is full of surprises. Shadow and light try to penetrate mother's abdomen and her endocrine system in shafts of uncertainty, but the wait continues. We realize on some level, even while in the uterus, that we are helpless and weak, subject to the past and to the future. Nevertheless, we are in the realm of the soul, where creation begins, and we are imprinted with the image of our creator. Thus, we sense as we enter the world that archetypes "demand to be taken seriously . . . they are [were] the bringers of protection and salvation, and their violation has as its consequences the 'perils of soul'".[7] And, as we can never successfully escape our archetypal foundations, it follows that mother, grandmother and the ancestral pantheon will be with us forevermore.

In other words, the archetype of the grandmother, who is our most memorable ancestor, next to parents, is our connection to the past. Ignore her and her steadfast influence, and we ignore the roots of trees, the stability of the self and the possibility of consciousness. Without her consciousness brought forward from the earth's inertia, we are the prey of fads and so become insignificant, disconnected from history and memory and any kind of synoptic view of humanity.

Grandmother, stepmother, even mother-in-law comes under the aegis of the mother archetype. Count nurturing friends, guru, Mary the mother of God, other goddesses, mother country, mother church and our longing for redemption, for a few more examples. Mother symbols abound.

During my last visit to Zurich as a student, I had a dream of mother and redemption. In my dream I lived in a house near the shore. The ocean beyond was blue and tied to the dock was my sailboat. Written on the hull was the name 'Redemption'. The blue ocean of bliss, the mother vessel and the proximity of my personal unconscious were close to my home. Therefore, what floated on the surface of my shadowy unconscious was becoming accessible. Darkness is not the only thing that lurks in our shadow. Sometimes it is our unused potential. The writing of this book is one of its manifestations.

My analytic clients, the ones who stay for long periods of time, are the ones who yearn for mother. To be a part of their journey is a humbling experience. My love of autumn, of the harvest, of the huge hanging moon just on the horizon, of the furrowed gardens and of the caves inhabited by bears in the mountains; all of these signify mother. When the image of mother accedes to that of grandmother, the archetype is larger, once removed from the birth mother and, therefore, a container of greater wisdom. The great grandmother "may assume mythological characteristics and elevates the archetype to a higher order or rank."[8]

As with all of the great archetypes, therein are contained good and evil actions. Mother is related directly to such actions in the present, but also in the realm of the myth. Good and evil are transformed into lessons on values and how to live life. It is here that the grandmothers are elevated in status. They can be blessed wisdom while being the devil's own. Little Red Riding Hood discovered that her grandmother was really a wolf in disguise that was ready to eat her up. Like Lucifer, who was once closely aligned with the light of the world, grandmothers, too, can become dangerous and sneaky forces for evil. For instance, a grandmother can use her wisdom to covet power. As for grandfathers, they too appear in my dreams. While I was still in analysis, during my studies in Switzerland, there came to me a dream of a wise old man. All night he led me up the outside stairs of an ancient tower. On the walls of the tower, carved in stone, were inscriptions that were translated, explained and dealt with one by one on our way up the stairs. Wisdom and folly were pointed out, mostly mine, but these were representative of ages and lives I had experienced and what I had learned. All night I touched on these insights imprinted on the tower. The delicate handholds they created impressed me and I somehow absorbed them. Each bit of wisdom had only to be recognized, like a final tally to be put into my awareness account. The old man and I worked together all night, and I awoke refreshed and renewed. This dream is another example of an ancestor, once removed, who acts on behalf of the great archetype. In doing so, the archetype retrieves and represents that collective place where all great and stored wisdom is derived. Grandfather's wisdom also reminds me that mother was forced to go out to work each day because father could not find employment. Perhaps it was written somewhere that I was to be the beneficiary of Grandmother's wisdom.

Sometimes the soul comes to acknowledge the devil side of the grandmother. She is not immune to deliberate and convenient forgetfulness. It is often the case that grandmother is perceived as channeling unconscious material through a whole generation. When consciousness skips a generation, it becomes the conduit of an older generation's unfulfilled desires. That which is not dealt with in one generation is imposed on the next generation. Now it is someone else's task and responsibility to solve. This would seem unfair on the face of it but is, in fact, the human condition that we find so twisted and tangled in modern times. Certainly, this ignorance is nothing new, for very few humans take seriously the psyche's task of untangling these ignored issues. The reason few wish to take on this task is because of the pain that is invited in, when old wounds are derided. Like physical wounds, emotional wounds must be exposed to the light or they will not heal. In order to embark on this voyage one must be determined to trust that psychic pain can be removed through this process.

Basic trust, of course, reminds us to circle back to the first chakra, that energy center of death and birth, fear or trust. We return to mother. In the first chakra, both Shakti and Siva are called upon as representatives of the mother and the father of the world. They join their respective opposite energies to infuse the new being with life. In so doing they inculcate warnings that advise us to use that energy to survive. These manifest as fears and limitations. At this level energy is tempered, a fire is stoked and the embers are stirred. Here, basic trust resides. At this level energy is neutral. It is neither good nor evil. Here is the full force of life, simple and pure. How we decide to use that energy, to cultivate our taste and to make our choices is what determines the quality of energy we utilize.

Stories, narrative and myths usually begin with 'in the beginning'. Grandparents or old people are most apt to begin their stories with this phrase. It would seem to be an attempt to leave nothing out of the tale. It is also a way to deal with the archetype, for the archetype can never be dealt with directly. Instead, symbols gather around an event or a person. They fit into a pattern or are explained in tragedies or through humor. In the process of story telling, symbols are organized or understood. They attach themselves to something that is already familiar. The mother archetype, while an aspect of creative consciousness, must come to us in a form that we can understand or with whom we can interact. How is it we learn to interpret new knowledge? First one fact is known, assuredly and most likely through experience. Then a new fact attaches to the previously learned fact and makes sense. As for the archetype, most of this attachment process or add-on understanding happens unconsciously. What is formed in this collection of facts and experiences is a cluster of concepts. These clusters can be made of understandings or misunderstandings. These cling together in a bundle: the greater the archetype, the larger the bundle. In psychoanalytic language this bundle is known as a complex. It holds itself together with cherished memories, experiences, hurts, misunderstandings, slights, insights and everyday life.

Archetypes, those invisible structures of the psyche, are organizational in their function. In the formation of a complex, they are a group of images and ideas that are readily accessed. The contents of a complex are not necessarily all bad or all good. They are simply collected, recorded and catalogued for future reference. Truthfully, it is how we perceive these ideas, images or energies that is most important. It is our attitude or our intention, as we come into contact with each of them, that reveals our purpose. As unconscious energy, the archetype takes on a life of its own.

Jung was fond of the following deceptively simple grandmother story. As guileless as it may sound, this innocent experience could well turn into the underlying basis of a complex. It began like this. "When a child . . . she [the narrator] had the following conversation with her grandmother:

"Granny, why are your eyes so dim?"
"Because I am old."
"But you will become young again?"
"Oh dear, no. I shall become older and older, and then I shall die."

"And what then?"

"Then I shall be an angel."

"And then you will be a baby again?"[9]

Such a story is an excellent example of the kinds of misconceptions we encounter in our daily attempts to soften our fears and to make sense of this mysterious life on earth. Although this story is charming, even enchanting, who can say if it is true or false? It might end up as the foundation of a misconception. It is certainly a narrative of comfort and relies on a belief in angels and perhaps in reincarnation. This is not to say there is anything amiss in such a telling; it is only to demonstrate how the most apparently innocent experiences change our belief system and may accumulate in time to form a complex. If one were to unravel and follow a single thread in the life of a fifty year old neurotic with panic attacks, that single thread might lead to a story heard by a three year old child to assuage the fears of death that might have concerned that child. Perhaps the real reason for the child's concern was the death of her mother or the family dog, and the child was temporarily soothed by stories of a grandmother who turned into an angel or a baby. In Jung's telling of this story the real issue was the impending loss of family for the child. The child's unconscious process emerged as a prelude to the divorce of her parents. In the end the child did much better when the parents became conscious of their own fears of separation and finally divorced.

Another and larger issue at stake in this small narrative is that of reincarnation or rebirth. Potentially, when one is reborn, memory survives from past lives. Life as we know it, via the personality, continues. In a sense each new birth is a chance to begin again, to heal transgressions and to redeem the higher self, which has been left behind. It is another chance to transform and renew the spiritual aspect of being. The confusion experienced as a complex, like a tangled ball of yarn, can require endless patience to untangle. Once again, we have all been mothers many times. According to Buddhist theories of reincarnation, everyone and every living thing has been a mother, even my own mother at one time. It gives one pause. Because every living thing was once your mother, honor her, nurture her, as she once nourished you.

If nothing is lost in the unconscious that means that our past existence cannot be denied forever. It means that what we have done or omitted doing in the past is written on the tablets of history and often feels like fate. It is said in the *Tibetan Book of the Dead* that in the process of dying and being born we are beset by illusions that will carry us into another incarnation. These illusions are what keep us from the terrifying visions of truth. This truth would be inseparable from karma, that reckoning on the truth tablets that denotes whether we will return as humans or in some other life form. For the Tibetans, for instance, it is generally acknowledged that evil and unconscious action will eventuate in reincarnation as a turtle. Why a turtle? Think how seldom the old turtle has a chance to be reborn. In contrast, children are revered and treated as precious, due to the proximity to their last life and the important insights they learned in that last life.

Think of it another way. Ask if the illusions of childhood, the reverence for the child, are derived from collective memories. If the child is a vessel of karma and a certain remembering that is of a recent past life, then that connection may need to be remembered for as long as possible for the sake of evolution. Such valuable information would benefit all of us, not just that individual child. If we could remember our past role as mother, there might be room for improvement. Surely, we would adopt a different attitude toward the role of grandmother.

Lao-tzu says of the Great Mother that she "was something formless yet complete, that existed before heaven and earth, dependent on nothing, unchanging"[10] In this wisdom we see formlessness and fullness, before and after, beginning and end, soundless silence and the music of the spheres. In other words, all that is big and embracing which contains, surrounds, entraps, shelters, preserves and nourishes anything little is part of the Great Mother. In our embryonic state we experience her best and idyllic protection as we are warmed, fed, comforted and blessed. In this round uterine environment we are still whole, undivided, inside the sphere, egg, circle of her body. She is plenitude and the origin of consciousness, emerging from the formless world. In her we make our transition.

The Great Mother is also depicted as many breasted, a provider who feeds the embryo and then the newborn. She sacrifices her own body to satisfy the hunger that accompanies new life. She nourishes "the first form of assimilation known to man".[11]

Nourishing by self-sacrifice is also the first act of conscious realization. Eating, digesting, and assimilating: from each of these emerges a sense of power over the outer world. In the Upanishad, Brahma, the creator whose heat assimilates the food of the mothers, is simultaneously acknowledged as one of the mother's gifts:

> From food all creatures are produced.
> All creatures that dwell on earth
> By food they live and into food they finally pass.
> Food is chief among beings . . . [12]

In this image of creation is the image of rebirth of mothers within mothers within mothers. Birth is the regenerative triumph of life over death. It is the food of life.

In my dream of bringing my mother into the sphere of Brahma, creative heat in the form of the little stove in the middle of the room was synonymous with the fuel of creativity. My misinterpretation of that dream in the early years was to think that it was literally my birth mother who had to be brought on board. This misunderstanding took me on a long detour and emphasized my repetitious efforts over many years. It tells me that the power of the mother archetype is all consuming at times, especially if mother's attitude is totally incompatible with that of her offspring.

Developmental psychologists often refer to it as an unfortunate difference in temperament between mother and child. The Chinese refer to this situation as Dao. One's Dao is either in sync with the circumstance at hand or it is not. If one is unfortunate enough to be in an out-of-sync situation, nothing will work smoothly. When a child does not experience a mother's love, consciousness is slow to appear. Thus, development can be stunted or even misshapen. When it comes time to separate from mother, this must be done on all levels. One cannot simply walk out of mother's house, as many street teens are wont to do, and expect real separation to have taken place. True separation occurs deeply, down at the archetypal level. Without such separation there exist confusion and conflict. Anger that springs apparently from nowhere, as problems of conduct disorder for example, exemplifies such conflict.

The journey taken to define the self, as separate from mother, is the hero's journey. If the origin of the journey is merely masked defiance, the trip is postponed until mid-life, when it must be approached on a more conscious and deep level. For those whose issues spring from maternal deprivation, it may take many years to begin a conscious healing, for how does one begin without a sense of direction or destination, without a home base or without the guiding hands of a mother? Acceptance is the key to healing. If not from mother, it must be found elsewhere.

In early myths that depict the hero's or the heroine's journey, we are witness to the all powerful and devouring parents who virtually eat their children, imprison them and subdue them. When the heroic journey begins, there is a ritual initiation that usually pertains to the most fundamental problems of life. To pass the initiation is to begin to understand the ultimate meaning of existence. When the mother parent makes demands, she must be appeased, and if the appeasement is not forthcoming or if mother is ignored, the child must pay a price. The young and heroic may be thrown out of the safety of the nest and into the unknown.

From the moment I arrived at Yasodhara Ashram, my inner journey to awareness began. It started on my first night, once again, with a dream. There appeared before me a huge spider web. Watching silently in one corner was a black spider. It was a warning that a dark and devouring mother inhabited the realm of my unconscious. Though I had ignored mother I had not escaped her or the role of scapegoat into which I had been cast early on. My self-exploration at the ashram in the years to come was also to be an introduction to my power as a woman. Fortunately or unfortunately, I had not had enough experience to know that the path I was about to step onto was that of consciousness. I stepped joyously and blithely into an exploration that became a great and fulfilling odyssey. The food I craved was the substance of mind and heart. By this time I was already a mother myself, but now I had found a mother substitute in the form of a guru, one I resisted every step of the way. How was I to know that my fear of another mother in the embodiment of a guru was founded on my own rejection by my birth mother? For some reason my highly honed survival system warned me to fear this important first step on the path of awareness. I would experience a similar fear as I began studies and my own analysis in Zurich. Not everyone is suited to this exploration, and many fall along the wayside, either bereft of courage or overwhelmed by unconscious contents that initially must be handled purposefully, then must be approached gradually and in a timely fashion.

Genuine fear is a defense mechanism and arises for a good reason. In the search for consciousness survival skills are important. So this was the price to be paid. This was the cost of consciousness, the daily toll that struck in moments of fear and an acknowledgement of that fear, then an acceptance of the origin of those same fears. If "the archetypal image of the Great Mother has been injured on account of . . . childhood experiences of [the] personal mother . . ."[13] that image can be projected onto others. So the scapegoat may begin to imitate the twisted or rejected mother image, rejecting others, being cold, moody and not genuine. This reaction is unconscious and reactive and it derives from a wounded psyche. The scapegoat, after all, is an archetype in its own right and is a receptacle for that which is rejected. It is not, however, the way it must remain.

I think of Ayaan Hirsi Ali, Somalian wanderer, whose life story reads like the triumphant journey of the heroine. In her book *Nomad* she escapes from the claws of mother and grandmother who have scapegoated their girl child. She is an example of the way it can be. As she runs away, she runs toward awareness. She leaves the rejected scapegoat back in her village and learns about acceptance. Slowly, by keeping her mind open, she is freed from deprivation.

The archetype is numinous in its light and in its darkness. Therefore, even the child who is subjected to the scapegoat route, as the container of mother's darkness, the closet for her hidden or cast off clothes, does not have to succumb permanently to that darkness. The rejection the child feels may be useful, especially if the rejection is directed only to the role in which that same conscious adult finds herself. The scapegoat is superimposed on the child but does not belong to the child who walks away from deprivation. Every child is indeed a divine child. As such, each child comes into this life in the presence of the great as well as the small mother. Otherwise, the great monster births a little monster that births another little monster. In the end the Divine cannot be overlooked. Within every new child is a small and mighty spark of light. Each child is assigned a human task that must not be forgotten or ignored at birth. In native myth a reminder is spoken or sung:

> A person with the Beginning gift of the Mind must always try to include his Heart in his decisions. A man can live out his entire life without ever finding more than what was already within him as his beginning Gift, but if he wishes to Grow he must become a Seeker and Seek for himself the other Ways.

Hyemeyohsts Storm, *Song of Heyochkah*[14]

The most important task for each child is to cherish that gift.

In Native culture grandmother is the keeper of the old, often lost, wisdom. The spark of light is not the exclusive wisdom of council elders or men who hold on to power. It is not the holder of the sacred white beaver pelt or the bundle holder of the white buffalo calf robe or the warrior who sun dances to the beat of drums. Instead, it is the quiet wisdom of bread and sage, moon time and childbirth. It is the moss bag that holds the newborn and the never-ending joy of procreation. When a grandmother on a reservation dies, grief is long-lasting, for the one person who did not judge, who accepted and loved the child's tears and smiles is the one who remembers and who is remembered.

We praise the "sanctity of motherhood"[15], and we try to exempt mothers from blame. Deviant behaviors as well as the dangerous and terrible actions of youth are rarely blamed on their mothers. Yet, it is deemed frightening when someone is allowed to develop his or her personality without guidance. Individual efforts, as such, are criticized as a departure from societal normalcy. What is it that we fear from individual efforts? Is it the possibility that darker motives might step forward to gain momentum? Is it, once again, a question of projection whereby those who have not done their work envy the work that has been done by one individual? Is it a desire for control over that individual who has stepped beyond the crowd? Is it envy of the fact that what is being sought and obtained is available to anyone who makes the effort or sacrifice to attain self-consciousness? From the moment of the first kick in the uterus, the child seeks a relationship with mother. "Speak to me mother. Are you there? Here I am, mother." Acknowledgements are essential to a child: without them children have been known to fade away and die. Mothers are present as witness to the little spark. They blow gently on the embers and soon there is a flame. We observe this in the endless enthusiasm of children who are loved and encouraged to explore life's new paths.

Grandmothers are not known for stealing their grandchildren's light. They know from experience that there is no light without darkness, and they even welcome the dark winter months, when it is time to rest, hibernate and gestate the soul. The one thing I loved in winter was the prism on the window ledge in grandmother's bedroom. Watery, grey winter light filtered through the window and projected or refracted light in spots of color throughout the room. On Sunday mornings I was allowed to watch quietly in this inner sanctum, as grandmother dressed before she set off at a brisk walk to church. On Sundays, as well as on special church holidays, it was required that she wear more than one dress at a time. To keep me occupied during her dress-up ritual, I am handed a little box of holy cards. These were her treasures and mementos, given out at funerals with prayers written in Polish on the back and decorated on the front with pictures of angels and saints. I touch each one reverently and see the prism colors of the rainbow speckle the bedcovers and the old trunk that came with her from Poland at least sixty years ago. The colors land on her pink bloomers and camisole, the silk slips and the frizzy permed-hair halo on her head.

Recently, I undertook a shamanic journey of a Peruvian nature. The journey lasted several days, each moment light-filled with beautifully intricate patterns that reminded me of needlework. These patterns came directly from the inside of the holy plant that was used to induce this trance state of lucidity. Divine Mother, holy one, our Lady: in the healing tissue of the earth, you still exist and are willing to care for us as long as we listen and cooperate. Because this experience was channeled through the wisdom and direction of a shaman, my intuition told me this was a feminine ceremony derived from the herbal knowledge of the grandmothers. My intention on the first day of my journey was to water my parched spiritual life. I had felt numb in my spiritual practices, uninspired and out of touch with my own inner spark. My insights during the ceremony were endless but one scene appeared quite profound. It was the realization that I had dismissed my birth mother from my life. What the holy herb showed me was an image of my own mother in the presence of her big sister, when she was very young. Her sister was mildly retarded due to being born prematurely. Her sister was born at home, nurtured with a milk dropper and warmed by a hot covered brick in her crib. In my vision there was my mother with her arm around her sister, imitating her slow behavior and speech because she loved her sister so much she did not want her to feel left out. My entire concept of my mother shifted. She, too, wished to be loved and included. To leave her out was to reject the part of myself that sought acceptance. The reasons for life's problems are often hidden. Truth is often so different from what we are led to believe.

Synchronicity gives us clues that help us to remain open-minded; these clues are aligned with archetypal consciousness. Synchronicity depends somehow on a parallel course of ideas and manifestations that are usually unrelated or non-directed. These ideas, in turn, amass in the unconscious, as yet unconnected. They come together in the same way that a complex is interwoven. We catch glimpses of events that come together in most unique clusters, as if to seek our attention. Generally, this happens in response to a wish or desire that is still unformed, a need that is genuinely unselfish or information that is sought in an open and receptive manner. Often our thoughts line up with an archetypal consciousness and we are able to notice similarities and meaningful events that appear together unexpectedly.

As an example, the Daoist *I Ching* is based entirely on recorded and observed synchronistic wisdom throughout history. The user of the *Book of Changes* asks a pertinent question that does not require a mere yes or no answer. The question is asked to elicit wisdom in the form of a cross pollination of ideas that already resides in the unconscious of the user. I may ask, "What will be the essential theme of this coming year, regarding my own development?" The answer might be number sixty-one. Number sixty-one is called 'inner truth'. The written attributes of the answer involve gentleness, forbearance toward inferiors, obedience in joy toward superiors. The answer evokes the image of a bird's foot over a fledgling or a gentle wind blowing over the surface of a lake. It suggests the power of light that enables life to be awakened. It invokes a heart free of prejudice and open to truth, open to the psyche without restraint. This truth may be voiced and echoed from the spirit and it emanates from the heart. It is done in humility, once superiors have been consulted. Words and deeds must be used cautiously if inner truth is to be honored. All of this comes from the above question and the synchronistic events in one's life that led up to such a question. It is really the nature of the question that renders the seeker more or less receptive to the answer.

Often synchronicity has been likened to being in the zone or in a state of grace, harmony and balance. In this state all seems to be well and truly in sync with the universe. Cynics refer to it as mere coincidence; skeptics want to be able to measure cause and effect; believers believe that the hand of God has something to do with these magical moments. Depending on one's outlook, the unconscious can be friend or foe.

Regardless of one's intellectual grasp of the unconscious there is an inevitable psychical consequence of our connection or disconnection to psychic phenomena. It is as if we can ignore it but it never ignores

35

us. Depression, fatigue, anxiety, physical health or disease: all are manifestations of unacknowledged energies and feelings that emanate from the unconscious through the body. Realistically, how else can the psyche make known its formidable presence? Grandmothers as shamans have been aware of this fact for as long as grandmothers have existed.

In the shaman's body the roots of medicine and psychic healing were born. Today, grandmothers as shamans exist in the four corners of the globe. In Mongolia, Siberia, Peru and Mexico, among the Inuit and the Yoruba, women shamans have tapped into the unconscious of the soul and the spirit as they go into trance and allow their bodies to take flight.[16] Through their trance states they are recipients of insights that they have brought back from their travels. In their state of sensory deprivation, brain waves are altered and are able to release energy that is blocked. The energy these women come in contact with, whether theirs or that of the person they are trying to heal, is often referred to as qi or sexual energy or Shen, which is known as spiritual energy. They describe maps of the body where the energy flows unfettered. This practice, in another form, is linked to acupuncture in Chinese medicine. All of this was known and practiced before formal medicine was founded in the West. The energy, whether sexual or spiritual, is accompanied by heat and the bliss of connection between the body and spirit.

Hildegaard of Bingin and St. Theresa of Avila spoke of their marriage to Christ. In a shamanic sense they allowed the spirit to enter their bodies where ecstasy is orgasmic and blissful. Women have always had the ability to experience such bliss in their primal connection to the process of birth and creation. During menarche or the process of giving birth, they begin to gather their inner resources and vital energy. All of these sources of energy spring from the unconscious, from the body and from the bodies of mothers and grandmothers. They may also be accessed through fasting with focus and vigilance. Today these shamanic practices are being remembered and re-energized. Women are returning to their shamanic roots, some tentatively, some fearlessly. Some women are being called through their dreams.

On a recent trip to Turkey I met with a lovely and kind village woman whose father had been a renowned shaman. People came from many countries to be healed by him. The previous year her father had died. In the family were several brothers, as well, but when I asked if anyone in the family had inherited their father's ability to heal she said none of the boys had been interested.

Sure enough, when she a young woman, her father had taken her to a local mountaintop. This spot and two other promontories in the area triangulated the boundaries of a healing space. Apparently this space was recognized as being watched over by three women healers of antiquity. During my visit, this extraordinary woman asked me to interpret a dream she had dreamed recently. In the dream she was supposed to turn around and face two scary and strong men who had followed her. Beautiful, celebratory lights lighted her path but she felt menaced. When I asked her if she knew what she must face courageously, she paled and nodded, yes. She had been under the impression, due to the strong influence of local patriarchal culture, that women did not and could not be shamans. I believe the two scary men were patriarchal concepts that haunted her. She was a grandmother and considered very wise by the entire village. However, she had not yet acknowledged her powers of healing. If her gifts stay hidden because of fear, it will be a great loss to the entire community.

It was not easy for me to lose my own grandmother. One day I walked home from school, and there she was, sitting on her treasure trunk, the one she had arrived with from Poland. She was perched at the foot of our long driveway, waiting for her daughter to pick her up. Mother had asked her to leave.

For years she had been my silent mother, my acceptance and ease, my example of gardener and caregiver, my warm comfort and solid foundation. How do children grieve the loss of such a person? No one in the house spoke of her any more. It was taboo.

My expression of grief took the form of an incorporation of what she stood for: church, church, church and stubborn independence. St. Mary's Catholic Polish Church became my real home. The chancel to the right of the altar nave, where Mary lived, became my personal haven from the suffering of the world and the dissonance of my parents' home. Here I could sit and breathe, then talk to Mary, who listened intently to every word I said. Candles flickered softly. They could be lit with a penny offering. I had no pennies, so I just knelt and watched Mary and the flickering lights of the offerings of others. Our talks might go like this:

"Hi, Mary. Are you having a good day? I'm not. I can't cartwheel like the other kids, turn up side down or go round and round. How come? I'm scared sometimes. Can you hear me? You look sad today. Maybe baby Jesus was afraid to do cartwheels. It's not your fault he couldn't learn. Maybe he was afraid, too."

I had come to love St. Mary's, as Grandmother had. Its niches and back stairways beckoned. Here I was loved. It did not matter that the statues were paint-chipped and gaudy, the pews scratched and worn, the stained glass badly designed. Here the nuns smiled at me as though I was special, and no one shouted or cried. We danced Polish folk dances, said our prayers in Polish and sang in Grandmother's native tongue. It was my inheritance, as was the light that glowed in blue and red rays through the windows that circled the interior of the church beside each of the Stations of the Cross. I sat quietly in the center of the church and waited to grow up.

What Grandmother left me was the ability to worship. She also left me her prism.

3

Mother Surrogates
& Symbols

The prism deflects light so the face of the Divine may be seen in colorful reflections and in missing pieces. Poets, friends, philosophers and gurus, all of these refract a tenderness that is absorbed as forms of lovingkindness. They express their love of creation. Some of them step up to the challenge of caring for a child.

When Grandmother, who was also my surrogate mother, was gone, it was fortuitous that someone stepped in to take her place. That someone was Maria. One day, as I walked home from school in the rain, listening to the sad tears on my umbrella, sloshing through puddles in my big yellow boots and crying because I felt so lonely and so sorry for myself, I heard Maria call to me from her parlor window. She invited me in for cookies and tea served in lovely old cracked porcelain cups. That was the beginning of her surrogate motherhood and my salvation. Maria's daughter had left for university just a month before and Maria missed her. I was lucky enough to be taken in and nourished. Children know when they are loved, and I knew that Maria treated me like a second daughter.

Maria was different. She had escaped from Germany in the company of Brunek who agreed to care for her and her child. She had beautiful paintings on her walls because Brunek was an artist, and she listened to operas and symphonies on a short wave radio while knitting her own beautiful clothes, curtains, blankets and shawls. She cross-country skied through the woods behind her house, and she took rain barrel showers, naked and outdoors, before she entered the house. Her flower garden had big, bright blooms and her vegetables and herbs were often dried and fragrant as they hung in the passage to the back door. I had never met anyone like her.

She showed me maps of Germany and of Nuremberg, where she grew up. She baked her own cookies and cakes with real butter, without boxes or mixes, and she listened intently to my stories after school. She even gave me a special handkerchief in which to cry. Since Mother worked full time in a factory in town, after a visit to Maria's I had only to get home in time to hang up my school clothes, tidy and start dinner. So for several years I stopped each day to see her, to sigh in relief, to feel special and to talk about my day. Maria was my friend and my adopted mother who infused me with courage.

Symbols, by their very nature, hold more meaning than we can understand at first glance. They allow us to see indirectly the nature of archetypes, like the reflections of light through a prism, and they are as close to the unconscious archetype as we will ever come. Symbols serve as a bit of protection between archetypes and humans, something like seeing the face of God through a veil. They are significant in that they lead us to look beyond our small selves. They also prepare us for the numinous or holy encounter, should we ever experience it. We do not need to go far to discover symbols because they appear to us through our everyday experiences and dreams.

Once we become aware of a symbol, it often appears to have dropped down from heaven. In fact, symbols are everywhere and we simply discover them. They help us to change our attitudes about issues that do nothing to aid us in uncovering or pursuing our purpose in life. Symbols help us to find our purpose, especially when that purpose is elusive. They return us to the level of reality. Without our acknowledgement of symbols, we are not in contact with the history of mankind or of our ancestors, thus we are not in contact with the accumulation of wisdom from throughout the ages.

Union with the unconscious through symbols is a healing event. A true symbol becomes archetypal when it attaches to significant unconscious content and connects the individual to his or her larger self. In a sense, this connection or realization puts us in the presence of the Divine as witness to the inner divine.

As an archetype, mother is numinous and powerfully holy. Therefore, there are many symbols that point to the mother archetype. *Faust* for instance, was Goethe's brave attempt to understand the force of mother. In Goethe's epic poem, Faust makes a pact with the devil, whereupon he is privy to the unholy wisdom of the mothers. This is given to him in the form of a key. The devil hands him a key and says,

> The key will smell the right place from all others:
> Follow it down, it leads you to the Mothers . . .
> . . . then to the depths! . . . A fiery tripod warns you to
> beware.[1]

It is devilish inflation and ego importance that convinces Faust the he can handle such an encounter.

The city, the underworld, the cave, the dragon, the ark, the church, the well and its water, the tree of life, the coffin, the cow, the cross: these symbols signify mother. The mother archetype is associated with other symbols such as garden and vessel, the rose, the magic mandala circle, oven, woods, cauldron and country. We are surrounded by her influence. Mother symbols also cushion our contact with "she who must be obeyed".[2]

In all ways the symbols that point to mother lead the way to her. Symbols momentarily replace her and express what the primordial creation wishes expressed in that shadowy underworld. Symbols are a kind of temporary surrogate mother. Because mother is of the archetypal world of creation and destruction, to be in her presence is to grow automatically and to become transformed in one way or another.

Surrogate mothers fill in the missing pieces. In Maria I was able to detect positive aspects of mother that I did not realize existed. She offered me affection, peaceful receptiveness and an interest in creation. Flowers, food, music and art were her passions. These were absent from my own house, so I soaked up every hour I was able to steal in Maria's presence. It was my most secret life and one that I knew, instinctively, must not be shared.

My other life was spent in church. As church is a symbol for mother, it is no surprise that I became attached to my church activities from the moment I was dropped off there to prepare for first communion. Until that time I had never encountered the inside of a church. It began in the church basement. Communion classes were held there, as well as catechism and prayers, Polish folk dances and songs. There was even the Polish alphabet. My first friends, Jimmy and Loren, attended the same classes, and we were allowed to walk there alone from North School Elementary. The nuns who taught these classes treated me with great kindness.

I was fortunate to have these influences in my life. However, I know that creative fantasy that derives from the psyche can "arise spontaneously and without any outside influence"[3]. Despite the fact that modern philosophers have tried to demystify the psyche as merely part of the imagination, the psyche continues to exist and to find ways to express itself and to make itself whole. If the mother archetype, for instance, cannot be found in the sphere of the birth mother, the mother, if she is needed, may appear spontaneously. Maria appeared one lonely autumn day in the rain in New England. It was enough to make me a believer.

The essential qualities of a surrogate mother are as follows: giver of sympathetic attention and practical wisdom, helpful guardian of secrets, vital nourisher and mythic authority. These, of course, are some of the positive attributes assigned to mother. In chapter six I will discuss in detail the demon or negative aspects of mother.

It is the positive traits of the mother complex that have been glorified in novels:

This is the mother-love which is one of the most moving and unforgettable memories of our lives, the mysterious root of all growth and change: the love that means homecoming, shelter, and the long silence from which everything begins and in which everything ends.[5]

Thankfully, we relieve mother of such an inhuman burden and eventually use her good nurturance to stand tall in the outer world.

One of mother's very important tasks is to instill routine. From routine, discipline is encouraged gently, for without discipline the best plans may never happen. She teaches us to overcome inertia. Once our catechism class had made its first communion, we were required to attend mass every Sunday. This gave me leverage over my parents who had never attended church in my lifetime. They were shamed into going to confession. When I made my first communion and attended mass each Sunday, they attended mass. Such is the tyranny of the innocent child. Secretly I knew that my parents were no angels and needed to confess their sins. After all, I was nearly nine and all-powerful. I craved a discipline that would make sense of my life.

From the cocoon of the basement, the mother cave within the mother church, the communion class ascended to the main church as a procession of little angels. There, Mary looked on with approval. For many years I carried on my conversations with her because essentially I was a solitary child. She holds Jesus on her lap, and he looks too heavy for her. He is nearly naked and dead. He is, we are told in catechism class, her only begotten son though I am not sure what a begotten son is. However, it is obvious to me that Mary is sad but determined not to let Jesus slip out of her arms. When I talk to Mary, her eyes never leave mine. They are intense, trapped in the mask of a statue that is unable to play or to go anywhere. I try to visit her now and again just to keep her company.

"Mary, I'm here."

"Oh, there you are. You haven't come to visit in a while."

"It's true. There's homework and . . . did you notice me singing in choir?"

"I know you're busy and I have heard you singing. I'm glad to see you."

"You must get tired of standing there all day, alone. I really would like to visit you more often. Did you hear my prayers last night?"

"I did."

"Well, then you know I am going to give up on the violin lessons. The orchestra scared me. There were so many sounds and notes to count, and I did not understand when it would be my turn to play. All the other kids seemed to know what to do except me. Mom says 'give it up' cause I was never good at it anyway. Did you hear me?"

"I did."

"You don't say much."

"Not much. I like to listen to you."

"Did you know I just got a 'D' in geography?"

"Yes."

"Don't you care?"

"I love you anyway."

"You always say that."

"It's true."

"But my teacher says only smart girls like her daughter will go to university. She got an 'A' in geography. But I don't know where anyplace is except Germany, where Maria lives. I just don't understand maps."

"I love you anyway."

"Sometimes I think I'll never be able to leave home or to visit the wild animals of Africa or anything else, because I don't know where to go or how I will get there."

As the years go by, I am admittedly lonely. So I spend all my time at St. Mary's and come to love the nuns. Sister Bernadette frequently gives me a hug or has me run errands. Notes go back and forth between the church and the convent, and I am often asked to carry them. At the convent the living room is austere and peaceful. White lace curtains and a crucifix, healthy watered plants and a stiff-backed chair are about all the objects in the room. But I can stand, waiting patiently, for a long while for an answer to a note. I like it there, and I like the privilege of being singled out to carry important missives. That year, I am chosen to sing a solo in choir: "Most Beautiful Mother".

Symbols, like the church as mother, reflect needs that we are not necessarily able to voice. Of course, the church is filled with dogma and other rules and requirements that seldom miss their target, despite unvoiced or unfocused pleas. Jung admitted that, "if symbols mean anything at all, they are tendencies which pursue a definite but not yet recognizable goal and, consequently, can express themselves only in analogies. In this uncertain situation one must be content to leave things as they are, and give up trying to know anything beyond the symbol."[6] As a child, I certainly did not analyze my attachment to the church.

Today psychologists often excuse the mother figure for psychological disturbances in a child's life. Jung, however, believed that mother "always plays an active part in the origin of psychic disturbance . . ."[7] especially if it dates back to early childhood. Apart from the birth trauma, there are numerous opportunities during childhood for psychic injury to occur. One of the most likely times is the birth of a second child. If grandmother or a precious and trusted nanny is present, these injuries may be alleviated. Otherwise, mother must work on her own state of consciousness. This is not an easy task and certainly not everyone's chosen path. Much of the time in our current Western society mother goes out to work and leaves her child in that group void called a day care center. While there can be no doubt that these facilities hire those who do their best to occupy children in playful activities, there is no substitute for mother. There are age appropriate emotional developments that must occur in a very small child. The first task to master, however, is trust, in the secure and loving arms of the one person who is bonded to the child.

As the first task that must be undertaken in life, establishing trust is the most important. It is mother who imparts that sense of trust. She does not let the infant fall or snap its neck; she feeds it from her breast that lets down milk whenever it is needed; she keeps the tiny form warm or cool and regulates peace and quiet for the essential sleep needed for the child to grow. She smiles and speaks to the little person in her charge and, best of all, she bonds with this new human spirit.

But the sad truth is that many of the babies conceived in our fast-paced modern world are not wanted. Many of the rest are merely tolerated. Mother has maternity leave, and her baby begins to talk back. Suddenly the infant is not wanted as much as mother thought it was wanted. Now mother realizes she is attached all day to a needy person. Meanwhile, the need for trust, the first and fundamental mastery of life, continues. Trust, expectations, even faith in the power that sustains life, is incubated in the first year. Will this child expect life to smile or to frown? Can it expect to snuggle near a breast and be fed or to be left in its crib in wet diapers and solitude? Will it expect to cry and be picked up and comforted or will its cry be a pitiful whimper of sorrow? And what of the circumstances that may be inevitable, such as a difficult birth, followed by pain for the mother, or an inability to nurse?

After World War II the trend in hospitals and among doctors was to use an anesthetic as part of the birth process. This "innovation" rendered mother's role minimal and she did not remember her great stake in bringing forth her child. After the birth, it was not uncommon for mothers to be told that they had not enough milk production and therefore must bottle-feed the baby. Whether this was by mutual consent, so that the returned war veteran could spend more time with his wife, or because the medical world truly believed they were being helpful, is anyone's guess.

Libido is a primal, non-sexual energy. It is called upon in the early part of the life of an individual as the source of the drive of creation. It is kept in a reserve from which the artist or inventor, immersed in an introverted state, is able to extract material from the unconscious for a work of art. It is a return to memories long forgotten, a descent to the underworld, where the mother image regains importance and upon which the paradise of this infant state is drawn. The work that is done at this level is virtually a miracle:

> Oh as I was young and easy in the mercy of his means
> Time held me green and dying
> Though I sang in my chains like the sea[8]

Note that "Fernhill", by Dylan Thomas, refers not only to early childhood, but also to the primordial time before then, when the foetus floats in the womb-like sea. This unconscious memory is the one still connected to the source of all creation in a collectively held bank of time. Thomas knows that when he was born he was meant to die. That is his destiny and ours. He may sing in his chains but freedom from mother is a delusion.

As libido is another word for energy, what is released so miraculously from the body and the mind is the energy necessary to do creative work. It releases the wisdom that calls from the depths with a longing to be heard. Without those unfettered yearnings nothing is heard, no motivation exists. The music that composers compose, the epics that writers write, the colors that artists see: these are merely glimpsed before the artist descends to the depths to retrieve them in full. In my own case, creativity has appeared in the form of echoes. We all experience a glimpse of the creative world. For many there is a fear that accompanies the call or the echo or the glimpse. The fear is that of the great unknown, the mistrust and suffering we are not sure we could endure. For Dylan Thomas there was a mystical acceptance of the cycle of birth and death.

What we know instinctively is what Faust found out. Danger lurks in those depths in the realm of the mothers:

> When the libido leaves the bright upper world . . . it sinks back into its own depths . . . and returns . . . to the mother, because from her the current of life reaches us. Whenever some great work is to be accomplished, before which a man recoils, doubtful of his strength, his libido streams back to the fountainhead—and that is the dangerous moment when the issue hangs between annihilation and new life.[9]

At this moment of choice, most choose to stay in the bright world they know, as opposed to the world of the so-called devil they do not know. Fear takes over. Is it also fear of the early mother, the untrustworthy circumstances the newborn found as a welcome to this world? As it turns out, one must find courage to go down to that dangerous place of the mothers. For one of two things can happen there: the person can become trapped and devoured or, conversely, the person may love it there so much that he or she does not wish to return. Either option is dangerous, destructive and untenable.

The underworld as a symbol of mother, that place where Faust fears the presence of the mothers, is well known in the myths of the gods and goddesses. Persephone, the daughter of Demeter, lives there. Persephone visits the earth's surface each year, leaving the home of her husband Hades. She ensures that spring returns and seeds are planted, that crops grow and are harvested. What would we do without her great benevolence? Growth is her specialty. She is the effort it takes to grow. As the daughter of Demeter and the wife of Hades, she sacrifices her comfort, otherwise known as inertia. To do so she rises to the earth's surface, leaves home and oversees the work of creation.

Inertia, one of the major symptoms of depression, is one of our major fears. We need to know how Persephone extricates herself from her family. Perhaps she finds a surrogate mother in nature: Mother Nature. One has to look at the gentle rain that falls in spring, the placement of the seeds in furrowed soil, the attention to the sprout, the weeding of the plants, the harvest and finally the act of eating. Attention, gentle compassion, attention, care, more attention and patience: these must be Persephone's qualities for half the year. The other half is spent with family in the dark and restful time that regenerates and renews the effort to care once again. This is the perfect approach to depression: gentleness, self-compassion, attention to goals both small and large, patience with self, and finally, gratitude.

The act of eating what the goddess Persephone has caused to grow is an act of gratitude for her work and sacrifice. Often in depression there is overweight. Inertia and ingratitude are deep states of sleep. Without attention, patience and compassion, there is no gratitude for the food eaten. There is no focus on gentleness or kindness, either. There is very little wakefulness at all. Food is used to anesthetize like using sleeping pills. Food that is not blessed and revered and thanked turns into a poisonous sleeping potion.

Just after my own daughter was born, I met a woman who became another surrogate mother to me. Her name was Sylvia Hellman, also known as Swami Sivananda Radha. Her teachings in kundalini yoga were gentle and made comprehensible for me by her clear and practical approach to life. She became my guru or spiritual mother. As such, she became my personal guide, my teacher and helper in the process of my spiritual transformation. Whenever I was troubled or perplexed, I drove my car from Calgary across the mountains into British Columbia to Kootenay Bay and Yasodhara Ashram. There I learned of gratitude, forgiveness, acceptance and myriad other esoteric understandings that must be experienced before being understood. She was my teacher who taught by example. I learned to distinguish truth as a part of reality, apart from fantasy.

Swami Radha's writings about hatha yoga demonstrate how the yoga asanas or poses are symbols or archetypes. Her book *The Hidden Language of Hatha Yoga* investigates these physical postures in relation to their symbolic meaning. The mountain pose, for instance, symbolizes standing still, taking a stand. It is "a symbol of the aspiration to transcend one's little self"[10]. It is also a symbol of the Great Mother in the form of Cybele the goddess of the world mountain. Symbols are hidden in our everyday speech, in our actions and in the objects with which we surround ourselves. Swami Padmananda, one of the teachers at Yasodhara Ashram when I was a student, encouraged me to surround myself with symbols of Divine Mother. Even if they became nearly invisible from day to day habituation, she advised, they would work on my psyche, my personal unconscious and finally my level of archetypal awareness. Today, every room in my home has some reminder of Divine Mother. For years they have given me comfort.

The first time I visited Yasodhara Ashram, I took my four-year-old daughter. It was the middle of summer, and we ate our meals outdoors beneath shady apple trees. I had been there a full day and had yet to see Swami Radha. When I saw her approaching along the path from her private home, I saw that she was accompanied by other swamis and followers, all wanting to share a moment of her time. Suddenly, my daughter jumped off the picnic table bench and rushed toward Swami Radha. She was shouting to get her attention and stopped in front of her to block the path.

With little fists on hips my extroverted child demanded to know, "Are you the grandmother, here?"

Brought up in a stern Germanic household where children were most likely seen and not heard, Swami Radha stared at her and simply said, "No, I am not." It was a standoff. Then Swami Radha asked, "Why do you want to know?"

"Because I want you to *do* something. I have no one to play with," my child cried out before turning on her heels to rejoin my table. In her wake I could hear the grownups gasp.

Later that evening, as I was reading a bedtime story to my daughter, there was a knock on the door. I opened it to find a beautiful young woman who asked if this was Clea's room. My daughter looked up in interest. Swami Radha had sent this gentle and fun soul to be my daughter's personal babysitter for the remainder of the ten-day course I attended. My daughter, filled with anticipation about the next day, fell asleep instantly, with a smile on her face.

The image of the guru, whether male or female, is the image of the surrogate mother figure. Once a guru, who is basically a bodhisattva, makes a commitment to teach a disciple, there is a bond between them that is eternal. The bodhisattva is said to be an enlightened being who sacrifices the immediate joys of heaven and promises to return to the state of embodiment to help other humans. The sacrifice, though very human, is synonymous with Persephone's yearly return to the surface, where she cares lovingly for the earth. Thus, even in death, the guru's job is to continue to help disciples and to teach and love compassionately. A beloved part of Hindu as well as Buddhist belief, the bodhisattva as guru is an image of mother, a symbol of the succor and teaching necessary for spiritual growth.

One particularly famous guru of India, who was, coincidently, a woman lovingly referred to as 'The Mother' comes from Pondicherry in southern India. For years this woman was part of Sri Aurobindo's ashram, beloved by its residents and the community for miles around the ashram. Considered saintly, a recognized bodhisattva, she told her followers that walking beside Divine Mother throughout our life is the most important thing required of each of us.

Sri Aurobindo was her greatest devotee and was, himself, a worthy sage. Despite the fact that The Mother was very much a real woman, she was revered as the embodiment of Divine Mother. Spiritually enlightened, she emanated holy wisdom and grace. She protected her children and loved them compassionately. Sages and sinners flocked to touch her robes and be healed. In her eyes was surrender to the larger good, as she allowed herself to be a conduit for healing and inspiration. She referred to Divine

Mother at all times, seemingly entranced by the next life, which seemed visible to her. In the Christian tradition she is a Mother Theresa who tends to her sick children. In this case The Mother tended to sick souls.

I went home from my encounter with Swami Radha and started a hatha yoga practice based on what I could remember from yoga classes. It helped ease my troubles and perplexities but loneliness persisted, as did a feeling of exile from the past and from my own body. It was not so much family that I missed as the landscape of childhood. I longed for the forest and the hills of the New England Berkshires, the colors of autumn and the spring flowers that drank in their spirits during downpours. I recalled the summer days deep in the woods, lying on fragrant pine needles and dreaming of my ancestors beneath the ground. They sang to me from the rocky circle I had found in the woods and they recorded my deepest secrets that were not to be shared with anyone. I longed for the winding roads and the funky old houses, the grouchy neighbors and the old graveyards. The earth, I realized, had been one of my surrogate mothers. I took out a journal and began to write, and what wrote back and touched me was my own poetry.

Suddenly my daughter looked happier, a friend appeared, I was asked to join a dream group, and then one day we were able to put a down payment on our first house in a friendly neighborhood.

Any archetypal symbol is dual by nature. That is, it is made up of opposites. There is a dark side and a light side intrinsic to every image. It is wisely noted that without the darkness light is not apparent. In a more helpful sense, if the dark side of a symbol is all we have encountered, then the light side will become recognizable by contrast. Eventually, this contrasting difference will come to our attention through forces of attraction. Opposites attract and come into contact with each other.

This moment is one of revelation. The more conscious one becomes of the presence of the other, the more bound one becomes to the other side. Thus, understanding is born. The alchemists, who once mixed the elements of dark and light in the symbolic form of real metals, were constantly in search of the bonding substance that would combine natural ingredients to create a new substance. Most of them took this task literally and became chemists. The ones who understood their task metaphorically became philosophers. The element that binds opposites, we know today, is love. Love is stronger than any of the opposites. The alchemists referred to it as gold.

The mother who gives of herself and continues to give without concern for her own replenishment, whether surrogate mother to many or just to one, is typical of the bodhisattva except she is only human. This type of woman is not as rare as we think. Recent Internet think tanks of women with breast cancer have revealed that they share a common quality: they are women who have continued to give until they are depleted. These are the superwomen who nourish, whose breasts have finally emptied. Symbolically nature frowns on this imbalance and steps in to change the balance. It is part of the larger balancing of cyclic opposites under the aegis of Mother Nature. "Here are my daughters, giving too much," she says. "Now, they must be forced to learn to receive." It is the other side of the archetype, the bigger picture of cosmic balances and scales. This overabundance of maternal giving is an unconscious phenomenon. It is a submersion in the archetypal unknown, on a level referred to by Carl Jung as *participation mystique*. At this level generations of unawareness congregate to keep awareness at arm's length.

The attributes of a *participation mystique* resemble a disintegration or dis-ease that has no shape and that upsets the unifying tension that binds the middle together. It is a primordial swamp in which opposites nearly disappear, and in which the person is easily lost, overpowered by "the archaic forces of the unconscious".[11] Once again, there is a resemblance to the place of the mothers, the descent into hell or a night sea journey beneath the shadow of death. It is a place where only the hero or the heroine goes and comes back intact. Many recovered breast cancer mothers have made the journey.

The term *participation mystique* means mysterious and mystical experience. In the atmosphere of analytical psychology there has forever been an aura of dread and fascination in connection with this observation. For Lucien Levy-Bruhl, philosopher, sociologist and ethnologist, it conjured a magical need to refer to all the stars in the heavens to explain the progression of a disease. The term attempts to define an occult state that may resemble catatonia and psychosis on the outside while the inside churns in the depths of hell. It proves the saying of Philippus Aureolus Paracelsus, early alchemist and healer, that "disease comes from the Father,"[12] not from rational man, but God or Goddess. Only cooperation with heaven can lead to health. Thus, the psychologist must be guided by heaven or no treatment will come to any favorable conclusion. In other words, the therapist must believe in the power of the Divine to heal.

If the symbol of Mother transforms to the greater archetype of mother, it is done through a yearning to reach heaven and to connect with God. Meanwhile, the mother complex may loosen its hold and create poetry or any other form of art. Mother is now no longer merely the woman who is a channel for my birth, she is the Great Mother whose energy holds the earth together, and she is persuaded to release a share to me. Primitive man or early man feared this struggle. To alleviate fear, communal sacrifices were offered to unburden the intolerable terror and heaviness of having to undergo this journey alone. Christ, of course, was the willing sacrifice who shouldered this burden in the hopes of doing for others what they were incapable of doing alone. Thus, he became an intercessor to the heavens. Yet, it was his personal mother that he left behind on this journey to the Creator. On a parallel note, the lone poet gives up his or her connection to a smaller mother, as well, if he or she intends to leave behind the fearful influence of mother to ascend to the realm of inspiration.

The Persian poet, Zoroaster, tried to make this journey alone, transforming his private collection of knowledge into a grander and more universal knowledge. When he sacrificed his small, earthly self, he found his larger self. His is the hero's journey expressed through the philosopher poet Friedrich Wilhelm Nietzsche in *Thus Spake Zarathustra*. As a hero, he exclaims, "Piled with a hundred burdens, loaded to death with thyself, a knower! Self-knower! You sought the heaviest burden and found yourself.[13]

Zarathustra's words could just as easily have referred to the task Christ undertook on the cross. It could also refer to Zarathustra's personal and symbolic gospel of the superman, of the journey of a poet who dared to look into the serpent pit, into the cave of darkness, into the coffin of the corpse. All these domains belong to the Great Mother. The poet heroes relinquish their burdens through the sacrificial rite that leaves mother behind. It is a dramatic departure.

Participation mystique, when it does not completely absorb and overwhelm the individual in the form of a psychosis, usually comes with an intensity that is unexpected and emotional:

> So it is not surprising that, when an archetypal situation occurs, we suddenly feel an extraordinary sense of release, as though transported, or caught up by an overwhelming power. At such moments we are no longer individuals but the whole race; the voice of all mankind resounds in us. The individual cannot use his or her powers to the full unless he [or she] is aided by one of those collective representations we call ideals, which release all the hidden forces of instinct that are inaccessible to the conscious will.[14]

The *participation mystique* dips into this collective unconscious to elicit help from ancient ancestors to create a work of art or to extract some other form of wisdom and energy that arises through the body and the instincts. It goes there to form our ideals, as well.

This book is my journey into Psyche's realm of the soul, and I know fully that my task is surrounded often by darkness, by steep cliffs and by loneliness. I say this because I am not the type of person who expects to change peoples' lives. I am the type of person you would not notice on the street. Exploring as a child, I struggled; coming to grips with being a young woman, I attempted to escape; plunging into motherhood, I often sat at home waiting for a phone call, a cheery voice or someone to remember I existed. Those calls were rare. Then, there were the doctor's appointments, the plumber's visit and the mason's repair work to the flagstone steps, the diaper service, and trips from car to house with groceries, car seat and baby. Do not forget the baby. Quiet sips of tea revived me. As a treat and a source of vicarious adventure, there was the phone call to an old friend in hopes of adult conversation. Most often, no one answered. Friends, too, ran errands and hoped for calls, did not return calls or did so when their need to hear a human voice was desperate. Mostly, what I remember is that I needed to remember everyone around me until I forgot myself.

Hopefully, I have been a good mother to my own daughter. I look back and realize that it truly matters that, except for the grace of Divine Mother, my mistakes and troubles would have amounted to disasters. My life has been rich in experience. My days are so full that I must take each one in hand to appreciate fully what I have been given. It has been said that any part of life left unreflected has not been lived. It is my ulterior motive, for this narrative, to scrutinize my life and to reflect on its refracted angles. That way I can learn from what I have been given to redeem my life. Otherwise, my mind that wanders could turn into a wandering mind of wasted opportunity and ungathered, scattered moments.

I see as beacons of light the surrogate mothers who entered the early years of my life, souls who came to care for me, to love me and to demonstrate to me that love appears in many forms, that it often appears when least expected, from people who know what love can mean to a child. Grandmother came all the way from Poland, Maria from Germany and then Swami Radha from the land of bodhisattvas.

When I sat before Mary to pray, I do not remember speaking prayers or making devout wishes. I sat and waited in awe, listened and waited in silence. When occasionally I asked other mothers to show me the way, there was always an answer. For instance, when I was dazed by the needs of my own daughter, Kathleen appeared. She became my friend and subsequently my daughter's second mother, her very own surrogate mother. When Swami Radha seemed bigger than life, someone I did not wish to bother with more everyday neediness, Lisbeth re-appeared, a cloistered Cistercian nun who became my spiritual friend and shared with me her most intimate dilemmas as another woman and as a humble saint. Recently, Damlanur, a woman who practices meditation, entered my life to revive my health and positive spirits.

I have so much to be grateful for, especially for the grace and good will of so many surrogate mothers.

4

Other Mothers:
Churches,
Crucibles & Rituals

Houses of worship are great containers for holy mother. The energy of anima or soul collects in sacred spaces—even those spaces on a page. Anima is a part of Divine Mother and her sanctuaries.

As the years went by, first communion was followed by confirmation. All of my friends were from St. Mary's Catholic Church and we were in the confirmation class together. We linked arms and marched through the church basement singing, "I am a soldier in Christ's army". I became a leader among children, sang in the choir and took communion each week, wearing my beautiful blue veil and Sodality of Mary medal. Mary's color is blue, the color of the sky and of the lapis lazuli stone found deep within the earth.

After confirmation I joined the senior Sodality of Mary and a Polish folk dance group. With ribbons on our skirts, long hair in a crown of braids and black patent leather shoes, we twirled in dance with cheeks flushed. In choir, the chorus, under the direction of organist Elizabeth Asklar, sang as loudly as possible while Elizabeth played with arms flailing and feet dancing along the organ pedals. "Sing out. Sing," she cried, "We are closer to heaven up here, and God can hear us!" We sang with great elation, as every note soared into the ears of God. That was the thing about being in church. The only times voices were raised, they were raised in song.

Even surrogate mothers need homes in which to abide. For me in those early years the nuns were my surrogate mothers, my family, and St. Mary's Church was my second home. The nuns shaped my value system and set an example of peaceful industry. The church building itself was a source of peace and inspiration. Beneath the vaulted ceilings and curved naves my soul found solace. Here was protection and the rhythm of routine. Here were flickering candles and mysterious shadows. It was not frightening; it was mysterious in a way that brings to mind inspiration. It is no coincidence that the church is referred to as mother church.

We give our institutions names that denote their power and that are descriptive beyond more than conscious awareness. It is the collective that chooses our descriptors. In this instance the church captures the energy of mother in both her terrible and her benign aspects. Great Mother meets monument of worship, meets vaulted and majestic space, meets parental security under the care of priests who call themselves fathers. Yet they dress in the long robes of mother. All that is really missing is an actual mother but her presence is everywhere. I could feel that presence in the church repository of millions of prayers, supplications and devotions.

Mother substitutes include the church. Her symbol is particularly relevant to "those not born from the fleshly mother but from the symbol of mother." In such forms individual energy can find an outlet, be useful and attain "a level of consciousness higher than before."[1] This fact is welcome for those who virtually are raised by surrogate mothers. As one of those surrogates, the church has embraced many converts: priests, nuns and the homeless. Mother and church are beyond all doubt connected. When a child detaches from childhood, detachment from mother follows, and the mother archetype acquires a different relationship with the individual. In many cases that substitute relationship is with mother church, otherwise known as *mater ecclesia*.

At age fourteen I am forbidden to see Maria anymore. There is something inherently wrong with this command. As a teenager I have begun to make my own decisions. I have a summer job, working in the tobacco fields as a laborer, and the only one willing to be seen with me, as I get off the bus after work, is Maria. My clothes are blackened with nicotine, my skin stained and my hands cut. I look tired and miserable, and Maria waits at the corner so we can walk home together. I am so grateful for her company and for her support. That summer, despite decrees from home that forbade my visits with Maria, I found many ways to appear at her doorstep for a cup of tea and comfort.

At fourteen I wanted so desperately to leave home that I took a job in the tobacco fields for the next two summers. It was grueling work, and my day started at five in the morning. I jumped out of bed, dressed, made a lunch and ran the mile to catch the yellow school bus that drove us to the fields forty-five minutes away. Work began at seven, beneath agricultural nets that became steam baths later in the unrelenting heat of the day. The other girls who worked there were a tough bunch and older than I, but I had found out that one as young as fourteen could get a job in agriculture. Though I was afraid of the girls who taunted me and called me crude names, and of the Puerto Rican men who worked in another section of the fields, I kept it well hidden. The men lurked around the sheds at lunchtime, making crude suggestions and offers. They carried machetes and threatened me with one on a day I mistakenly went to the other side of the shed to eat my lunch in the shade. When I stood my ground and told them I would see them in hell if I were attacked, they backed off and seemed quite uncomfortable. After that, I realized it was some ritual form of bravado and bitterness that drove their behavior. I asked them if their mothers knew what they were up to.

Several weeks into the long summer, the bus driver, a teacher in the winter, insisted I sit directly behind him on the bus so he could keep an eye on me. He realized the older girls and their counterparts, the men, often threatened me but that I did not have the sense to back down from danger.

For two whole summers I baked in the sun from seven in the morning until four in the afternoon, and then had to be driven by bus to the drop off stop to walk home. When Maria met me I was covered in black tar, exhausted but determined to continue with the job. In two summers I saved the three hundred dollar tuition to pay for my first year at St. Mary's Hospital School of Nursing. I was proud that I had paid my own way, that I was strong enough to resist and to stand up alone, that I could defy the peer ridicule and the admission that we were very poor or that no one supported my wish for more education and for a better life.

There was an even greater reward for me in those two summers. I stood strongly in the soil and reached to the sun each time I strung a plant to the overhead wires. I brushed against the lush green tobacco leaves that gave off their earthy smell and sticky protection. I sweated in rivulets that dripped into the soil and I counted my breaths. There were moments I became so tired I thought I would faint. Through it all I never stopped moving my body while my soul grew lighter and lighter. My skin was tanned, my muscles honed and my strength grew each day. I loved the tobacco plants, their little shoots, their magnificent verdant leaves. Through their stalks I felt the sacred earth. Today, when I have been to a Native ceremony and have given tobacco as part of the protocol of gratitude, my soul remembers the plants and how they once helped me get through a day. At the same time I remember that the blue sky, vaulted and vast, was like an outdoor cathedral but more intimate. There my voice was heard through the soles of my feet and was lifted up. When I stretched up and hummed a song to the universe, I was heard deeply. There was no question that I was not heard. My inner song was healing and made me feel whole.

For the child looking separately, first to mother then to father, there is great division and confusion. As the years go by there is less time before and after class to visit Mary but I still hurry up the back stairs that are used by the altar boys and the priest. These secret stairs are a shortcut used by Mr. Stanislavski, who keeps the mops and brooms beneath the stairway, and by the nun who changes the flowers on the altar. Kids are not supposed to use these stairs but it is obvious to everyone that the church is my home away from home. So no one minds.

It seems that Mary is everywhere: her icon is in the vestibule; the Pieta is to the left of the main altar; the standing Madonna is near the chancel raised high on a pedestal. The black Madonna and the white Madonna mingle, though no one mentions the words black and Madonna in the same breath. She is simply Our Lady of Czestochowa.

Several girls in the Sodality suddenly express an interest in becoming nuns. In eighth grade we still go to catechism classes together and have just made our confirmation but I never suspected that they had vocations. So we are all driven together in a group to the Convent of St. Joseph in Enfield, Connecticut for a visit. The next evening I announce at dinner that I, too, wish to join the convent. To me, it seems like a brilliant solution to escape home. I am met with great opposition and ridicule.

Opposition becomes my middle name at this stage in my life. The violin, visits to Maria, ballet lessons, possibilities and potentials: my mother rejects these outright. In early photos I stand there without a smile, eyes sad. The chance to live at a convent can be interpreted easily as an escape route. It was simply not to be.

Opposition derives from opposites and from our dual identity. There is church and state, mother and father, dark and light. Life is a constant series of opposites, contradictions and paradoxes. What that means, essentially, is that opposites will always appear because they exist naturally. The tension between opposites, however, if in suspension long enough, will create a third option, a solution. Then, if we are patient enough to wait in such a perfectly balanced and suspended state, that third option will be a creative event we have never considered, for that is the formula out of which chaos creates.

The third option or the solution to our problems, as C. G. Jung would express it, comes from the waiting, alchemically, to add another element to a dual situation. That element, one of the many special gifts given to me by Maria, was an introduction to Mother Benedict of Regina Laudis Abbey. It happened in my senior year of high school after I had earned my driver's license. I offered to take Maria there secretly, in my father's old three-cylinder Saab. The Benedictine women's abbey is located in Bethlehem, Connecticut, and it turned out that Maria had made an appointment for me to meet with Mother Benedict, the founder of this monastic cloister.

I was enchanted with the place. Its tiny chapel invited peace while inciting in my mind a longing for possibility. The forge where some of the nuns worked at their sculpture, the gardens where flowers were as important as the fresh vegetables, the little gift shop where artistic labors of creation were displayed, alongside books by Thomas Merton and Teillhard de Chardin, the lunch we were served in silence that was vegetarian and felt holy: all these facets of the community touched me profoundly. I missed nothing, as my senses searched like radar to take in the rich solitude of the atmosphere and the fact that the women there were encouraged to use their talents and their potential. I did not overlook the sculpture of Our Lady of the Hermits at the monastery entrance that somehow reminded me of the icon of Our Lady of Czestochowa.

Then Maria, who was not even a Catholic, introduced me to Mother Benedict before leaving us alone together. This was a turbulent time in the Catholic Church. The liturgy was being modernized, priests were leaving the priesthood, and convents were nearly empty. Habits were being exchanged for ordinary street wear, and the religious were being sent out into the community to work for a living. The church no longer supported them. Mother Benedict faced this dilemma and asked me for my opinion.

No one had ever asked me my opinion about anything, so I took this request seriously. She asked me to come to the abbey for a retreat weekend, and the next week that was exactly what I did. I wrote poems on the questions she asked me about the future of monastic life, and I presented them to her. We talked for a long time. For some reason she listened carefully as she tucked the poems into her missal for further reflection.

As founder of the abbey, she had arrived, alone, in the United States just after World War II, settling in a country whose language she did not speak. She learned English, as she went from door to door in order to raise money and interest in a Benedictine order of nuns. Support was slow in coming from the Vatican and obstacles presented themselves at every turn.

It was obvious that the new trends of modernization and apathy were not a part of her vocabulary. As she tucked away my ideas, which had to do with maintaining tradition, I could feel the powerful energy this woman possessed, energy that manifested in a belief in the church and in the role of monastic life as a vital contribution to the path of devotion.

So strong was her devotion to the purpose of the sacred cloistered life as a path and as a secure place from which to light up the world through prayer, that I became a believer. This was the aspect of mother church that was true, a place of return to the basics of keeping in touch with the soul. It provided a space out of time, a center of light in an ever changing and often disturbing world. Here the hours of prayer and work, whether in the fields or at the forge, were long and arduous.

On the first night of my retreat I was awakened for matins at two in the morning. Bells rang out in the cold night air and frost gathered in the trees and on bushes. Silence penetrated an icy fog and stung lips shut. Hush, it seemed to say. I looked up at January's barren tree limbs and noticed in awe that they were being dressed in a mist of frost. Yet one branch stood out from the others. It formed a tiny cross, laced and frozen in place. Its arms reached out in such motionless beauty that I stopped in my own tracks, to listen more intently to the prayerful silence. Then I noticed more and more of these little crosses. Had I not stopped and gazed upward in awe, I would have missed them. Moonlight touched each miniature cross like a blessed witness and I, too, witnessed this winter prayer of the living trees.

The worship of the cloistered nuns in this monastic tradition was alive. Highly educated and artistic women knelt in a life of prayer that was important enough to be given priority. Reverence for silence penetrated the gardens and the forest, the guesthouse and the chapel. Silence allowed nature to speak and to be heard. From that day my love of the monastic tradition with its mystical worship would sustain me throughout the dry years of wandering in search of my higher self.

Today, I continue to retreat to monasteries and abbeys to refresh my soul, to allow myself to sip of the crucible that is mother church, to taste of her goodness and to sleep through nights cradled in peace. Even the ritual of the mass is unhurried there. Communion is offered in a community of sincerity, and the Gregorian chant is an inspiration and expiration of the breath of God as mother and father. It is all so simple and so pure. The test inside the holy crucible is that of being at one with my own nature in order to discover its gold.

Primarily, the energy encountered at the feet of the mother archetype is of the anima or soul. According to Jung, the concept of anima is dependent on the mother image. In turn, the anima is refined by an ideal. In pursuit of an ideal, a woman looks for a father image to complete her inner life and to raise her creative spirit above her instinctual nature. The church brilliantly recognized this desire to fulfill ideals and so created marriage to the church for its priests and bishops. As for the women of the church, what was offered was a marriage to Christ himself in an otherworldly union of spirit and soul. What was not counted on was the eventual, all too human, wearing off of the ability to remain married to an invisible entity. The body of the church is really its people. Individual priests have suffered greatly in their inability to experience union with the soul through marriage to a real woman. As for marriage to Christ, women in the church are at an advantage. Mother church cares for and protects women in convents. A woman's spirit may take her on a journey of mystical bliss. For the congregation as a whole, mother church offers forgiveness and absolution of sins, reconciliation as well as communion with the body of Christ and with the whole congregation. As such, a man may leave his mother without ever leaving mother, and women may fortify their souls while keeping their spirits within comfortable confines through the mass.

Hildegard von Bingen was born in 1098. Her music has lasted for a millennium and appeals to the anima. Hildegard was a visionary and a healer. She was also the abbess of a community of monastic women, and she believed that "the body is the garment of the soul, which has a living voice". Her librettos give praise and gratitude to Mary's womb that gave birth to the Son of God. She refers to Mary as the "leafy branch"[2] from which fruit grows. Her liberated visions and her music resound today as the carriers of mystic knowledge acquired in prayer.

Brought to live at her monastery when she was only eight-years old, she was a gift from her family to the church. As a precious gift, she was treated to the wisdom of the mother superior of a medieval monastery who came to be her true surrogate mother in the church. She grew up virtually fostered by mother church. Born of a prominent family, she was taught at an early age to read, to write and to play music. As a sensitive child, she had visions that remained a part of her secret inner life. By the time she was forty and made abbess of the same monastery, she could not contain her visions. By this time she was strong enough and bold enough to insist on their veracity. The messages she received in her visions concerned compassion and love for the body that housed the soul. She frowned on the practice of self-flagellation as an offense against God's creation. She became a healer and an opponent of the immovable patriarchy of the church.

As the patriarchy is still very much present in the church, one encounters the father or male energy of the animus, as well. It is inevitable and natural that the opposites be present in any communal institution. The energy of the father resembles choice and reasonable knowledge that is obtained when children remove themselves from the influence of their mother. When this is accomplished, children begin a new life of awareness rather than of habit. In this world one cannot sit around and wallow in the energy of the mother for long. A break must be made and awareness embraced. The ideal situation, as referred to by Jung, the ancient yogis and the Buddhists, is self-realization. Here, finally, the opposites come together; the anima energy and animus energy that have been held in tension for years join in an alchemical cauldron to create a third that is a new direction. This union occurs as an act of love. However, it must be noted that alchemy is a patriarchal endeavor that attempts to extract gold from matter. The traditional form of extraction that occurred in the boiling cauldron was rather heated and harsh, and its purpose was to separate the gold from the grasp of the earth, a symbol of mother.

Children are always in search of the love that is the product of the union of anima and animus because children are the essence of that union. They search for themselves in the midst of emotional chaos. Thus, the church appeals to children. The stability of mother church, secure and routine, predictable and punctuated by rites that are timeless and transforming, is a remedy for disorder and chaos. However, awareness, whenever it finally arises from the unconscious, requires that the higher self take a stand and evolve beyond mere conventions and dogmas. The self must be free to explore and to choose its own path to individuation, unfettered by the rules of mother church. In this sense, the child grows up and eventually must leave home to secure a self-identity.

In reality there are those who stay forever under the aegis of mother church and who follow dogma to the letter. These believers emerge with great difficulty into full consciousness, for they follow strict guidelines for their entire lifetime. There is nothing wrong with such actions. In many respects this is the easiest path. There is no personal questioning or interpretation of right or wrong doctrine, no dark night of the soul in which one is lost to the mother, no loss of direction or rudder in rough waters. Confession in the presence of the priest, if done in the correct spirit, is done in the presence of God. Outside the church, however, you are on your own.

Today the church still takes seriously the care of souls but the modern world has intruded. The church is understaffed and stretched beyond its capacity. Protestant sects have created separations into many and diverse factions, and the motherliness of it all resembles, most closely, divorce in families. It is left to the psychologist to address the spiritual malaise that is most prevalent in society.

The truly good news is that, regardless of the state of institutions and dogmas, the voice of God can always be heard. When we take the time to listen, we hear it quite clearly. In fact, without mother church padding and protecting us from direct contact with God, it may prove difficult to ignore direct experiences of God on a daily basis. Without the intervention of the church we are left naked and exposed. Our direct contact with not only the spirit but with each other is inevitable. We are baptized, confirmed and married in the church. We are even buried under the sanction of the church. For better or for worse mother church directs and intercedes on our behalf. For better or for worse many willingly take refuge in the church their whole lives.

The church "gives expression to the unknown psyche of man through its rites and dogmas."[3] Without these rites and dogmas the western world is subject to its "own deplorable spiritual inferiority, which seems to have little resistance to psychic epidemics."[4] Without ritual where is God's answer to human problems? In our secular politics we have few answers. When we recognize, for instance, that politicians cannot live up to the burdens imposed by an electorate, we hopefully also realize that elected politicians do not have answers. Figuratively they are crucified for pretending otherwise. It is only through channels of enlightenment that answers can be considered honestly.

Without ritual we are also susceptible to possession, whereby the unconscious takes control of the individual. Church rituals act as intermediary absorbers of psychic content and redirect unconscious energy into more useful channels. It is often the church that investigates whether the source of this unconscious energy is good or evil, whether it is infectious or not and whether a healthy fear of this psychic phenomenon is appropriate. Symbolically, even the vestments of the priest are worn to maintain a distance from the unknown and the holy to protect him from the "immediate experience"[5] of God. Without defenses and seen in a psychotherapist's office, such vulnerability can look like panic, conflict, confusion, and depression, as well as indecision in the face of ethical dilemmas.

The Church, when it is an arbiter of discipline, demonstrates the finest marriage of masculine father and feminine mother. Once removed from earthly parents who have birthed the body of the individual, the church steps in as substitute mother with Christ the father presiding.

Once the church parishioner is of the age of reason, when personal habits tend to rule the body, issues known as the seven deadly sins appear. Inertia, known otherwise as laziness, sloth and gluttony which turns the body to fat, greed which translates to envy, covetousness and lust, and hatred which manifest as competitiveness, anger, false pride and hurtful behavior show up. All these vices reflect a desire to return to the dark cave of mother.

They act in opposition to the spirit of light. Our actions in the final accounting determine who we are. The tension between opposites requires a constant watchfulness referred to by mother church as the fight between good and evil. While it is not explained in quite this manner in psychological terms, there has been no better monitor of human actions created by humankind than the church. Discrimination, led by the powers of the psyche, accompanies a fairly high level of spiritual consciousness. Higher ideals and virtues are acquired through sincere practice. Church provides a venue wherein virtues may be exercised in an atmosphere of earnest.

Mary Daly, the feminist, wrote in 1978 of goddess murder, suttee, foot binding, genital mutilation, witch-hunts and the gynecological torture of women in today's societies. She wrote of women forced to endure false selves, confusion and the conditioning to pretense. She wrote of a woman's voice in the passive silence that describes the anima. What is feminine and who has pronounced what the feminine is to look like? The writer Virginia Woolf described the necessity to speak words in order to heal the anima. In *Moments of Being* she claims:

> I feel that I have had a blow; but it is not, as I thought as a child, simply a blow from an enemy hidden behind the cotton wool of daily life; it is or will become a revelation of some order; it is a token of some real thing behind appearances; and I make it real by putting it into words.[6]

In the conversations I had with Mary Daly we discussed such topics as choice, the power of words to be heard, and a voice for the soul or the anima. Later these same topics were to become paramount concerns for me. The decade of the sixties was a time when the Jesuits of Boston College tried to have Mary fired for writing *Beyond God the Father* while she held a tenured teaching position at their institution. Protest marches by students helped her to keep her job, and I was proud to have been a part of the protests. I considered her to be my friend. To think of women as marginalized within the church was a lot for me to take in at that age but Mary and I would attend plays by women at the Harvard Square Ipswich Church, listen to special lectures at Wellesley College and talk for hours. She was brilliant and on the leading edge of the women's movement. She wanted me to make something of my potential. She asked me what I wanted to do with my life, and encouraged me to think outside of the boxes in which women cowered. I began to imagine having choices.

Unfortunately, by the time Mother Benedict and Mary Daly had taken me under their wings and shared with me some of their understanding of growth and potential, I was already numb. If one is suffering from deprivation, which many of us are, we had to have got into that state somehow. For me, by then, twenty years had gone by. Birth trauma and childhood traumas that had to do with raising myself had already occurred. The arena of deprivation comes under the big tent of love, creativity, body awareness and educational expectations. When one has been deprived how does one realize what one has never had? It is a loss that permeates the defenses like a castle under siege, using up the last of its stores. By the time I met these women, my hunger was so great that every one of their words remains crystal clear in my memory.

Ten years later I was to meet Swami Radha. I was a new mother, far from home, alone all day with a new baby and no helpful resources or money. One of the first questions Swami Radha asked me was if I felt sorry for myself. My answer was, "Well, I believe I do." "Well, snap out of it," she returned. "There's no point getting on the spiritual path with an attitude like that. It's hard enough without self-pity!" I was quite taken aback. She had seemed like such a sweet old lady until that moment.

That mother church has been so successful since her inception is a tribute to the numinous archetype. In this case mother unites with father and therefore the archetype of the ultimate feminine unites with that of the ultimate masculine. Right now, the churches of the Christian religions are the largest and fastest growing phenomena in the Far East. China, for instance, now counts Catholicism as its largest population of churchgoers. The church derives from the archetypes of masculine and feminine in its collective image. The symbol that responds to our current pattern of behavior also responds to our needs. The church as a symbol of mother and father represents a deep need that relates directly to how much we seek union from division.

The primary symbol in the church is the cross that is also the tree of life or the mother. It represents the roots of wholeness. The tree of life is fruitful. It can be found in every one of the world's religions. When Mary, the mother of Christ, kisses the cross on which Christ hangs, she reconciles herself to death as well as to life. It is due to this mother archetype that the church maintains its vitality and mystery. As well, the church has, in its ritual, ways to collect the forces of the psyche for the benefit of good deeds, forgiveness, and conflict solving. Symbols are receptacles of the unconscious. The church is a dispenser of grace that leaves interventions in the arena of sacred ritual where it is empowered mysteriously.

At the level of soul work and the healing of souls, the church necessarily also provides for souls of the dead. The mass for the dead, for instance, is intended for the soul of the departed rather than for the congregation of the living. It provides a connection to history and to our desire to remember and honor as much of the past as we are able.

The church takes it upon itself to protect the individual, basically, from him or herself. Through the performance of sacred rites like the mass, the unconscious is kept in check. Members of the church community are safeguarded from any accidental descent into the realm of the mothers. Even Mary, venerated as the mother of Christ, is kept pure and blue-colored to constrain her in the realm of the sky and heaven.

How apt that mother church, whose central symbol is the cross that depicts suffering and the space between the heaven and hell of human struggle, should also stand for wholeness. The cross provides an answer to why we suffer. In oppressed countries the psyche cries out for such answers. Like all mothers who comfort their children, the church promises the comfort of answers. Note Michelangelo's Pieta where Mary mourns over the dead Christ. Has any culture surpassed this image of motherhood, so universally understood by every woman and man on earth? As a unifying symbol of the most powerful archetype imaginable, the church, with its curves and its protective interior, is surpassed only by its spires to heaven. Heaven and earth were both made for the Creator's glory.

One of the symbols that first spoke to me as a young woman was the mandorla, that form of oval that often encloses the figure of Mary or the saints, a feminine shape also known as a vessel. The vessel of fish, or fish and womb, were synonymous in Greek.

The mandorla symbolizes that erotic place where heaven and earth touch. When the two worlds are connected, as when two circles overlap, the polarity of dualism is embraced. What appears can disappear. Life eventually becomes death, and the great spindle of the weaver combines matter with spirit of Themis, the goddess associated with cycles of resurrection and devastation. We swim in the divine ocean of Themis. Her sacred day is Friday, chosen by the Catholic Church as a day to eat fish, a day that doubled as a fast day. She is feast and famine. Outside the church Friday was formerly known as a day of lovemaking, since fish is also known as an aphrodisiac. The sign of Christ happens to be the sign of the fish, and the Christ child has been known to abide in this mother womb that is in the shape of the mandorla. Mary's name resembles the many names for the sea where fish are abundant. She is a vessel for fish.

Imagine a valley between two mountains, the base of a flower, or Themis who controlled the cycle of the seasons and, therefore, law, order and divine justice. Themis was the daughter of Gaea, earth and moon mother, a Titan of the sea. Imagine two figure eights attached to each other, two mandorlas that symbolize eternity. Themis is aligned with the noble and pure swan maiden who is contrasted with the cupidity of mankind. To pursue her is to pursue a supernatural woman who is unassailable unless one offers gifts and accomplishments. This is no ordinary woman. She is untouchable, unavailable, unreal and put on a pedestal by men who have not accomplished the task of separation from mother. Jung was quite taken with the image of Themis and the anima. For Jung, this separation was an unusually arduous and heroic task.

The black stone engraved with the sacred laws of the goddess belonged to Themis, as did the symbol of her as the Mother of Prophecy. She gave birth to all things, including the new birth of mothers from the stones (read bones) of their own mothers. As a stone child, I knew that I had simply to keep searching through the bones of ancestors and their unfulfilled desires to discover what they had learned.

The mandorla encircled the figures on all the holy cards that grandmother shared with me each Sunday morning.

My search for mother would take me through Europe, into Africa and Tibet, across oceans and, finally, out west and north to Canada. Once in Canada, I realized I was in exile from my motherland, and I had taken one more step away from mother. Costly trips home were few, and what I came to realize was that I missed the landscape of my birth. Maria had moved away to live near her daughter. My siblings had dispersed to far corners, and people changed. Only the landscape remained unchanged. On one of my frequent visits to Regina Laudis Abbey, I met with the same frosted scene of the past, and once again I was entranced. This time Mother Jerome was passing by and noticed my awe. "They spend their days and nights in witness to creation," she pointed out. Suddenly, I knew the purpose of my whole life. To witness and give praise to creation is no small endeavor.

It was a revelation so profound it has not left me. It was the realization that never abandoned Zarathustra or Carl Gustav Jung. "Naturally we know by experience that the world does not come to an end when one individual comes to an end. But if consciousness comes to an end, then the world comes to an end—that is quite certain."[7] Who then will be here to witness the tree of life that grows and spreads its boughs? We know that Nietzsche was fascinated by and immersed in the mother archetype, the anima. His marriage to her was deliberate and complete, and for him consciousness came with great effort and understanding through his relationship to the anima. He was a poet and a philosopher, a grown man who had years and the complex genius of the artist on which to base his beliefs.

But what of the many thirteen-year-old girls who run away from home because they have no fathers and suddenly believe that mother does not love them? In this common scenario the teenage girl wants to die, she claims. "I hate her," is her mantra. For a child of deprivation there is no consciousness at all, merely blackness, darkness so profound he or she is willing to seek a mother in the underworld. Down there, surely will be rest and an all-enveloping mother love. Or will there be? Assuredly, it is self-destructive to seek in this direction a mother's love. Often referred to as hell, the depths could simply teach this child a lesson. If she survived, she might learn, like Zarathustra, that freedom and life are precious, not to be thrown away and wasted on a foolish whim. Life and growth come under the domain of the Great Mother; her terrible aspect oversees decay and death. Rites of passage are more safely observed under the aegis of mother church. The crucible or vessel of the church holds a teenager to ideals and values. Otherwise, the rites of the tattoo and the pierced flesh become tangible reminders of what is important.

Jung would say that the child's hatred is a neurotic fear that arises from the mother archetype, for in reality mother does live in her child. The hidden and secret life of the mother who perhaps recently lost her own mother and all helpmates or who perhaps has felt abandoned by her own mother must be taken into account. Mother is terrified; she cannot sleep and does not know how she will cope with life or with her child. Her daughter believes that mother does not really want her, that she is nothing but a burden. Mother becomes the fearful witch and ogre. Though these projections by the child seem fantastic, when they are unconscious they obtain mythic proportions.

How many children believe they were either mixed up at birth and handed to the wrong mother or that they have been sent into the woods to be eaten by a witch? In keeping with the mother archetype, the term witch originally meant wit or wisdom and has been twisted to denote hatred and heresy. "The Catholic church applied the word witch to any woman who criticized church policies."[8] As such, the witch is a negative aspect of the mother archetype, a part of the mother complex embroiled in ignorance and fear. While the psychologist may understand the birth mother's actions as anxiety or fear, her child may experience her actions differently.

Death by suicide can be a tragic consequence of this misunderstanding by children. Death is the desire to escape. The act of suicide takes this desire to a new level. How many children think to escape and how many adults live in an escapist mode? The absence of love is the greatest deprivation.

Adults, too, try to escape. They flee their homelands, go into exile, and find that they have to start all over again. We have all run from ourselves time and time again. In fairy tales children run into the woods and are cooked in cauldrons or ovens by evil witches. References to witches were used deliberately to scare children and to make them aware of the dark side of the mother. Some young women simply fall asleep and are anesthetized by the scent of roses and magic gardens. While trying to escape from mother we run straight into her arms, and then the work begins.

The writer Anais Nin spent an entire lifetime trying to escape from mother. She referred to herself as an escape artist. Subjected to sexual abuse at the hands of her father from an early toddler age, Nin was raised as a Catholic by French-Spanish parents. Her shame and guilt were hidden in the depths of her psyche, and her behavior took on a sexualized form of revenge. She defied guilt in a courageous attempt to defeat her shame. Her psychoanalyst, Otto Rank, advised her to confront her abuser with abuse, a kind of psychic revenge that nearly destroyed her life. She lived a life of exile, and her hatred of mother prompted her to abort half a dozen pregnancies, ostensibly to save those unborn children from pain. She wanted to protect them from the suffering of being born in mother's dark and exiled world. None of Nin's attempts at dissolving her torment was effective, yet one cannot but admire the courage she generated to continue her efforts to be well and whole. Throughout her life she never relented in her efforts to heal, no matter how misguided. Ironically, she died of cervical cancer, a disease of the uterus. The uterus is a mandorla symbol, one that is profoundly a symbol of mother and of a return to the womb.

It becomes impossible to run from mother. She is at home, she is at church, she is the ground beneath our feet and the country in which we are born. Jung once commented that the Catholic Church was in for many surprises when it assumed Mary into heaven in 1956. The Feast of the Assumption each August in Catholic churches around the world is a yearly reminder that Mary was elevated to the status of heaven. On one level it would seem that Mary was exiled from earth. On another level she has become a goddess, whether this was the intention of the church or not.

Anima mother, what do you look like? Here is her description from the litany of Loreto:

> Lovable Mother
> Wonderful Mother
> Mother of Good Counsel
> Mirror of Justice
> Seat of Wisdom
> Cause of our Gladness
> Vessel of Honor
> Noble Vessel of Devotion
> Mystical Rose
> House of God[9]

She looks like a beloved Beatrice worshiped as the soul of Dante. She is "the inner personality . . . the way one behaves in relation to one's inner psychic processes; it is the inner attitude, the characteristic face, that is turned towards the unconscious."[10]

On the outside, what the anima looks like can be hidden behind our outer face or the persona that we show the world. It is the completion of what is not apparent and "contains all those fallible human qualities . . . [the] persona lacks." For example, "a very feminine woman has a masculine soul [animus], and a very masculine man has a feminine soul [anima].[11] Thus, any qualities that seem absent in a person can be found in that same person's soul. We possess both an inner and an outer attitude. We try to save face, wear an opaque masque and cover up, oftentimes to hide the hurt and vulnerability of being beautiful.

We try to adjust to any environment. Sadly, if there is no correlation between our inner face and our outer actions, there will be many roadblocks on the path. Sometimes the inner soul image that is not expressed is projected onto another person. Most often, men project their soul image onto a woman, but certainly this process may work both ways. It is often the case, when a man does this in marriage, that he is now able to express completely his inner anima image while his wife is left depleted and bereft of her own stolen identity. It takes heroic stamina to withstand and define one's own soul in the intimacy of marriage. It is, perhaps, the reason so many marriages fail. Instead of dealing with the complexity of unconscious projections, it is easier to escape and to take the soul into exile.

Anima or animus: many children feel that they must choose sides between parents. It is an age-old duality that we need to understand to overcome. Church, known collectively as mother, is in conflict with those who wish to dominate her and who make rules to control her. The animus is the patriarchal hierarchy of the church, in the same way marriages, meant to be a union of male and female energy, become battlegrounds, sometimes with the children as foot soldiers on the front line.

As a child, I dreamed of Egypt and the Nile. I dreamed of a culture that is matriarchal. Years later, while on a trip to Ethiopia, I visited the source of the Nile. I listened to the ancient echoes that pounded in my ears as the waters of the Nile crashed into the canyon abyss that would take it north. I rounded a hillside corner in the mountains beyond the ancient kingdom of Axum and my heart stopped. As I gazed into the valley below, I knew I had been there before. I recognized every slope and contour of the land. An old woman was walking up the road in the same costume she must have worn five thousand years ago. I stepped over the ruins of the residence of the Queen of Sheba, viewed the hieroglyphic stelae on the ground and heard the hollow klesmers calling us to prayer in the town square of Axum. It was the month of Miriam, and I was invited to join the women in chanting before the dawn.

I had lived here before in this place where women were honored. It was during a time when Egypt was barely established, a time when the anima stretched over the land and it was fertile and sleepy. Women wove and buildings were close to the ground. The Queen's residence was small, as the foundation lines attested. Healing came from dreams and the advice of ancient ancestors. It was not a rational time, as we understand logic today. It was a quiet period of listening to the reasoning of the heart. Another woman walks past, nods in recognition and is gone. The children are beautiful, bright eyed and intelligent. In this hidden kingdom there was once the rule of mother. Later, almost all the cultures of the earth came under the rule of father. Back and forth the pendulum has swung.

Children feel great shame when they must choose between parents. They think that somehow they caused the separation. Immigrants spend many years justifying exile from their mother country, which they leave to avoid the violence, the poverty or the suffering of wars. Churchgoers feel empty and often guilty when they leave mother church because they can no longer accept the rules made by men. Right now, countless people are once again on the move to relocate and to find somewhere where the mother archetype is still at peace. Many are still hopeful of finding such comfort in the arms of the church.

Wholeness is the ultimate goal we seek when we implore the embrace of the good mother. Whether it is the symbol of the primordial circles of harvest on the earth, the talking circles of the aboriginal ceremony, the mandala-shaped cities of Tibet, the underground healing caves of Aesculepius, the clear water of underground springs, the forests of peace and reverence, the baptismal fonts of ornate cathedrals or blessings by the sea, we seek the wholeness that we recognize in the Great Mother archetype. We seek the beauty of her creation. We hold hands as we walk, and we put our palms together in amen. We seek wholeness and unity. In our churches and in our homes, which are gradually becoming our private temples, we try to acknowledge our gratitude and to whisper our awe.

5

Mother Nature:
Energy,
Evil & Experience

Our energy in the center of our being is ignited by the Great Mother, in the form of Mother Nature. Since ancient times, sages have invoked energy through yoga practices, drawing mandalas in the sand and in the heart of prayer. Buddha sat beneath the venerable bodhi tree to absorb mother's energy.

The twenty first century has begun with a new religion and a new myth. The movie *Avatar* sums it up perfectly in exquisite technicolor. It is the myth of an alien presence in another world. In the new world Mother Nature and all her creatures are revered and honored. The great church of this bright and beautiful society is the tree that represents mother, and from the tree all the healing energies may be accessed. The humanoid beings who live in this idyllic world are gentle and agile beings who exist in a fine balance with nature. In comparison, these exquisite creatures make earth humans look like savage and emotionless robots. Our war-like destructive behavior is crass and greedy; our machines depict our ignorance; and our level of compassion and understanding about our environment demonstrate a lack of finer feelings or conscience.

Mother Nature, we must realize, is not limited to this small space we refer to as earth. She is the whole universe. To know and recognize this fact is to begin to expand our consciousness to include the cosmos. This is a concept so old it has become popular once more, but like all fads, it is momentary, and we do not remember very easily what we already know. This is a concept and an awareness that we must take care not to discard like this week's headlines. With our short-term memory, we should be particularly respectful of cultures that still remember. Unfortunately, with our greed and insistence that modern ways are best for everyone on earth, we overlook past wisdom and ignore any consciousness we once possessed. We need to ponder the existence of Maya Angelou's caged bird and the reason it sings so clearly. We need to meditate on the rhythm of the heart in harmony with Zora Neale Hurston's dusty road and the four seasons.

What I remember most from the time I spent in Africa is the mothers and their complete devotion to their children. For years after, I dreamed of them. In the dreams they were always walking down dusty track-like roads with their children perched on their backs. They walked in stately, dignified rows as their children rode in wide-eyed wonder. While they swayed to the rhythm of their mother's hips, her hips moved in sync with bare feet that connected to the earth. Acceptance is what comes to mind. Their connection was to the whole world, to the ancestors beneath their feet and to the sun that woke them each morning.

For many years after my experiences in Africa, my dreams were peopled by black women. One of my favorite books was Maya Angelou's *I Know Why the Caged Bird Sings*. It was an enigma. What a strange title! Surely, it was satire. I bought a canary and listened to its song. I hated that bird for being so stupid, until the day I understood that its message was one of acceptance.

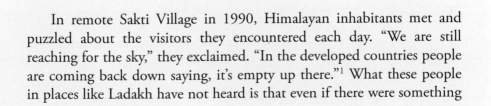

In remote Sakti Village in 1990, Himalayan inhabitants met and puzzled about the visitors they encountered each day. "We are still reaching for the sky," they exclaimed. "In the developed countries people are coming back down saying, it's empty up there."[1] What these people in places like Ladakh have not heard is that even if there were something up there we would destroy it because we do not know for what we are searching. We would not recognize it if we saw it. The movie, *Avatar*, is a clear warning of this possibility.

Carl Jung wrote a book about UFOs. It was written in his last years, and the gist of it was that these fascinations of humankind with life from afar would constitute the religion of the next millennium. The reason he gave for this prophetic pronouncement was his belief that we had used up all the numinosity of our present holy archetypes on earth and were desperately searching for replacements.

We do not live well or easily without our higher selves engaged in the quest for wholeness. This quest involves the evolution of our souls and our senses so that we may prepare ourselves for the future, whatever it may be. Whether this involves unidentified foreign objects or beings who have tried to contact us or to lure us to another planet is beside the point. The importance lies in what this phenomenon symbolizes in terms of a new mythos and a new dimension of reality for those on a spiritual quest.

So what is the purpose of our life? Is it true that in reality the great and terrible aspects of mother give us a push to instigate that inquiry? Are we being nudged to contribute somehow to the evolution of understanding and consciousness? Everyone says, "But what can I do? What can I offer?" I, too, asked helplessly. Look around. Can I nurture my own child with love and acceptance? Do I smile at my neighbor or shovel his sidewalk? Do I sit in peace and quiet each day to witness the wonder of the world? Do I hurry to watch violent games in stadiums and on television, or do I pay artists to play beautiful music, to paint the stars or to twirl their bodies in the ecstasy of space? What do I choose? Do I need to live in a big modern house, alone, with five thousand square feet of private and lonely space or do I rebuild a little house and bow to the welfare of my friends? Do I walk in the woods, listen to the rustle of leaves and pray from my heart for parents and for leaders or do I criticize continually? What do I do? Do I need to live in a little birdcage before I come to be in my own skin?

We have become afraid of Mother Nature, and that is because we do not like the fact that she is in control. We demand perfection; she is messy and delights in chaos. It is the basis of her creation. Furthermore, she is bigger than we are, knows more than we do and is more powerful. Without her we cannot survive. Does that sound familiar? Spoiled children do not like their situation, and all children try to get their own way. We simply think we know better than our mothers. Ask any teenager. Ask any scientist. They, too, feel that they know better. After all, did not most of them get excellent grades in school, win scholarships, receive the best education? We are so miniscule compared to Mother Nature and still we resent this fact. We are so mysterious and beautiful that we forget we are simply one of her myriad creations.

Experience is accompanied by waves of awareness. One minute we are on the crest where we can see all the way to the horizon; the next moment we are in a trough, phobic with the possibility of being doused by tons of water. We wallow in suffering. It is the nature of the terrible mother, the one who punishes us for our refusal to move out of the dark and into the light. For thousands of years the Buddhists have said that sorrow and suffering are here to stay unless we do something about them. Christians are a little less optimistic. They say that original sin is the first imprint on our soul from which we will not escape. The philosopher Arthur Schopenhauer added his own insight when he said:

> it is absurd to suppose that the endless afflictions of which the world is everywhere full, and which arise out of the need and distress pertaining essentially to life, should be purposeless and purely accidental. Each individual misfortune, to be sure, seems an exceptional occurrence; but misfortune in general is the rule."[2]

How ineffably sad is his comment. What we do not recognize surrounds us. The unknown is in the faces, the eyes, the glances and the smiles of our partners and of our children and of our friends and neighbors.

After living in the Sahara desert I went sailing. This contrast is a good metaphor for life; so is sailing. There is no other experience quite like it.

Until the day I set foot on a boat to sail across the Atlantic Ocean, I had no idea what I had let myself into. The sailboat was forty-one feet long; the crew was my newly wed husband and his parents; we set sail on my twenty-seventh birthday on a voyage that would take twenty-seven days. To make matters more difficult I had no idea that I would be seasick for the first seventy-two hours.

Curled up on my bunk in a tiny space that resembled a dark cave, empty and dehydrated, nauseous and weak, time meant nothing but endlessness. So this is the reality of Mother Nature in her mighty and terrible aspect where she drowns and then devours her children. There was no turning back. The sails remained set in the trade winds that howled continually. Let me admit it; I was scared. Not only had I never sailed or been on the ocean, I had rarely ever been sick from anything. For minutes at a time my mind would detach itself from my body and my thoughts would take flight, far from the churning of my gut and the smell of my vomit. I imagined black slaves in the holds of creaking old ships, submerged in the darkness of fear and the unknown, powerless in the face of nature and the shadow side of human nature.

Miraculously, after I had spent three days in mute suffering, I sat up, then stood, then made my way to the companionway to stick my head outside. This is what Lazarus must have felt like when he returned from the dead. I thought I was in heaven. The fresh salt air and the clean white clouds all around, as far as I could see, were glorious. I wrapped myself in a blanket and just sat in the cockpit, breathing in the blessed air and sky. This was the crest from which the horizon was visible, and I was going to live after all. The boat was like a cradle, and I was newborn in a way I had yet to understand.

Truly, this experience was a connection to Mother Nature, one we rarely are privileged to know. In our sophistication we have removed ourselves from her power. Out on an ocean hundreds of miles from shore, we know for certain that we are in her hands. We cannot fool ourselves.

My senses were alive to every nuance of her being and every breath in my own body. Experiential knowledge is truly the only genuine kind.

Recently, I visited the Galapagos Islands. I spent months before the trip immersed in the writings of Charles Darwin. I turned pages of Tui De Roy's *Galapagos: Islands Born of Fire,* a colorful photographic journey through her motherland, having had no appreciation for the fact that humans could also inhabit these islands. The journey was one that captured the joy of seals, the intense meditation of iguanas, the ingenuity of finches and the enduring patience of turtles. They live on volcanic islands still actively in the process of transformation. Intense fire, powerful waves and burning sunlight bombard the shores of these lava outcroppings to shape what they will become. The interactive forces of nature are so noticeable in this sanctuary that we stare in awe. No cathedral can compete. Anything we do is an imitation of the creation, destruction and sustenance of nature. We can do no better.

Darwin has been criticized for one hundred fifty years for his receptivity to these evolutionary energies. Adherents of the biblical description of creation blame him for our exposure to the work of Mother Nature and call him a usurper of God's sovereignty. Yet Darwin may have been more in awe of creation than most of his colleagues and friends. Imagine the moment of realization, when Darwin was witness to life that was living in balance with its environment. Imagine his awe and reverence at seeing the dance of creation, the immense energy that worships each new day. None of it, certainly, could possibly negate the existence of a supreme creator who orchestrates all these miraculous life forms and their reliance on one another.

From Mother Earth we get our energy. In kundalini yoga interpretations there is always a chart of the chakras or energy centers that are depicted as located in the body. Jung had a huge chart of this kind hanging in his office in Kusnacht. At the C. G. Jung Institute by the Zurichsee a map of the seven energetic locations is shown in colorful images. A goddess represents each of these locations; each goddess manifests the vast potential held in each symbolic center.

Like any archetype, the goddess Shakti, for instance, represents a certain kind of energy. Symbolically, the chakra centers are depicted as hierarchical energy manifestations from the first to the seventh level of energy in a continuum along the spine. This is not to say, however, that any particular energy center is more important than another. Trust, as an emotional energy in the first chakra, for instance, becomes acceptance in the fifth chakra. In the yoga system, knowing the location of the energy centers in the body helps us to direct the focus of spiritual energy. When energy is at a low ebb, it can be raised to a higher level through yoga practices.

Our body-mind is like an oil refinery. We can extract crude oil or grade-A fuel. It is our decision; it is our potential; it is also our own evolutionary path. The nature of kundalini yoga is spiral and literally travels up and down the tracks of the spine in a sinuous and parallel action. From pure ego in the first chakra, the energy ascends to the higher self at the crown of the head. These pathways allow energy to be controlled and cultivated, refined and used whenever intention or attitude direct it. As such, yoga practice may refine states of consciousness throughout the body. States of mind from humility and fear to power and pride can be released in this closed system, so awareness and directed intention are of utmost importance. Energy is neutral. It is what we choose to do with it that is important.

The goddess Shakti is considered to be the mother of human nature. It is said that Shakti was the one who became the word. Words are earthly manifestations of energy, and the mind delights in wrapping itself around each one. Mother of words, Shakti collects them in clusters until meaning is made manifest. From words in clusters we arrive at archetypes and complexes. One word attaches to another until a new meaning becomes manifest, similar to the way experiences related to each other attach to form a complex. So a complex is not all bad, and a cluster of words takes on a different meaning from the single word units that compose the cluster. Meanings change and grow and evolve, and we learn more and more. Eventually, the meanings of clusters may lead to a discovery of purpose. Of course, we must be looking for a purpose in order to find one or it will pass us by. We must be seeking and refining continually. We do this by asking, once again, "What is the purpose of my life?" then we listen and watch. We ask, "What makes my life worth living?" Then, we listen and watch once more. We do not make assumptions or take for granted the answers that appear in myriad forms, camouflaged in ordinariness. In kundalini yoga we dialogue seriously with our own questions and their most certain manifestations. We are grateful to Shakti for making inquiry possible

What are relevant in the study of yoga are our attitude and our receptivity to the divine within us. In the tree pose, for instance, we stand and copy the patience of the tree of life, a symbol of Divine Mother. We root ourselves on the ground and reach up to the heavens to connect with energy. We become receptacles of the energy available to us whenever we sit in awe beneath a tree or in meditation.

Remember the Buddha as an example. He received his revelations beneath the Bodhi tree. Remember Christ. On the tree of the cross Christ was redeemed on behalf of all humankind. If we still do not get the message or keep our minds clear to understand concepts that have gathered in confusing clusters, there is the headstand. This is a kind of reverse tree pose, where our feet become rooted in heaven and our heads are planted on the earth, the more likely to be able to hear the wisdom of Divine Mother. She whispers from the earth, and our self-centered thoughts are turned upside-down. Now we may see the other side of an issue. Often the insight comes in the form of a word, sometimes an image, and we become balanced once again. In this position we are very close to the truth and there is nothing else to do but listen. Otherwise, we become disoriented and lose our concentration.

Jung was fascinated with what he had learned from his friends, the Indologist Wilhelm Hauer and the sinologist Richard Wilhelm. What he discovered in discussion with them was the Eastern version of developmental aspects of higher consciousness. Jung believed that, through yoga, but especially kundalini, the East would come to understand the West and vice versa. For the West, the knowledge gained would help us to understand the mind and body in relationship to mental health. It would help us by giving us tools to develop spiritual awareness. Yoga, in the final analysis, is oriented to the individual's understanding of natural archetypes. The western approach to spirituality is primarily a communal understanding.

Yoga, we forget, is an ancient spiritual discipline, and through it "we also recognize a sort of religious rediscovery of the mystery of women".[3] The chakras, as viewed on kundalini charts, depict the energy centers located symbolically in the body in order to guide visualization. The visualizations are reflections on these energy centers. Energy equals Divine Mother equals Shakti. They are one and the same. When Siva and Shakti unite in the mind or sixth chakra, the personality is transformed and a state of bliss is experienced. The reason is because the lower energies, the ones associated with fear, survival, choice and discrimination have been channeled upward through the heart and into assimilative centers of the brain and the master pituitary gland. Metaphorically, the masculine and feminine outlooks reach an understanding in the highest, most refined energy levels.

Mother Nature has not forgotten the importance of destruction. We find her in the forms of Kali and Durga. Even in the West we find her in the form of the Black Madonna. We must step aside while fires burn, volcanoes erupt and mudslides descend to the sea. Keep out of her way. Who are we to start forest fires, to spend whole days on the craters of volcanoes or to build houses on treeless coastlines? Surely, we cannot expect our unfounded hysteria when we do not get our way to be given serious attention by Divine Mother. She has her work to do and we had better stay clear, respect the work she does to keep up on this planet and adjust our expectations to respect her great and restorative actions. It is a question of trust, trust in Mother Nature.

The goddess or Divine Mother has both negative and positive aspects and it was not until Jung's travels in India that he came to understand "a more lasting effect of [the] . . . impression of destructiveness of Kali . . . [this] was the emotional foundation it gave him for the conviction that evil was not a negative thing but a positive thing."[4] How, for instance, could we get rid of false concepts and move on in life if not for the process of destruction which in the West we usually refer to as evil? Basically, evil is a concept that needs further and careful examination in our culture. We confuse it with destruction. Without destruction how can obstacles be eliminated? Without destruction we accumulate more and more and begin to hoard; without destruction there is no autumn followed by the cleansing influence of winter.

When we practice yoga we acquire the tools to access the energy of consciousness. In our culture Hatha yoga, the approach to yoga most known in the West, is treated like physical gymnastics. It is used to keep us in shape or to stay flexible and it is often practiced in conjunction with some more aerobic form of exercise. Yoga fads have come and gone in the West for over a century, yet rarely is yoga utilized as a sacred tool. This is because in the West we tend to ignore the intelligence of the body in favor of the brain. We think that unless we can articulate certain knowledge verbally or examine its veracity under a microscope in a scientific manner, it does not exist. Therefore, the body's intelligence is not given credibility. Despite the fact that the science of yoga is over six thousand years old, we refuse to acknowledge its importance. Furthermore, it makes us uneasy. Many fundamentalist churches in North America attribute its existence to the devil. We fear what we do not know, and we refuse to know what it is we fear and ignore. Even those who have tried yoga may suddenly become wary of what they experience, as the body literally begins to talk to the conscious mind. The body, of course, stores all kinds of experiences that it has had, and like the proverbial elephant, it never forgets. After all, what would we do if we suddenly uncovered our trapped energy?

Mircea Eliade noted in his study of yoga that "we have no intention of inviting Western scholars to practice yoga . . . or of proposing that the various Western disciplines practice yogic methods or adopt yogic ideology."[5] Hauer, in fact, claimed that the practice of kundalini yoga examines the polarity of power that belongs to the mother and father, or male and female archetypes. Westerners who touch on this psychic awareness must practice kundalini yoga with a teacher who guides them beyond this point. Otherwise, they remain immersed in the body's unconscious contents in the realm of the mother.

The rewards for those who pursue such awareness are great indeed. Self-acceptance, realization of potential, freedom from self-limiting concepts: these are all benefits. Those who accept this challenge choose to scale the wall that is the ghetto of survival and begin to live. For anyone who has ever wished to be realized, there is the persistent urge to be centered, individual, as well as unique and separate from the crowd. Jung referred to this superior calling as individuation. Think of it: it is the same instinct as the one that tells us to leave home, be free, begin our own house building and find our own special path. It is also that separation of us from mother and her collective force of unconscious behaviors. As much as we may love mother and, thereby, Mother Nature, we have always sought our own roof rather than the branch of a tree or the cave on a mountainside. As contradictory as it sounds, this is our desire. This urge is as powerful as that of the couple who also wishes to unite and become one. First, they must learn to separate.

Chakras or energy centers in the kundalini system are also known as mandalas. As a mandala, each chakra is an energy entity unto itself. Remember that each center is not merely part of an ascending scale of energy; each one is no better than the one before it. Rather, each chakra is a circle and represents wholeness. Each is separate from the others and may constitute a single focus or path in itself. Hauer defined the chakras as "symbols of the experience of life".[6] As such, each one is creative and powerful as a foundation to our existence. However, it is said that in order to go from one chakra to another, we must do so in a night journey, a crossing of the waters, so to speak, motivated by excellent intentions. This is not a comfortable journey, as anyone who has ever crossed a sea must know. Fear follows us and we must make the journey alone. In a sense this is our true baptism. If we are fortunate, grace accompanies us so that, when a storm passes over our little vessel, we may not drown. Instead we are ever aware of a small flame, a spark within the heart that not only keeps us afloat, it transforms us.

In the heart center, or fourth chakra, the physical and the mental converge. It is here that we begin the awareness and appreciation of our own values and unique personal goals and images. We even see Mother Nature from another point of view. Though we may still prefer a roof over our heads, we begin to see Mother Nature's branches as beautiful and cooling. They become a shelter of wishes fulfilled. The tree is not a symbol of running or escape because the tree is rooted in nature. It is not a symbol of immobility or imprisonment either, for the tree that is rooted most deeply in the earth reaches the highest into the heavens. Technically, up there it absorbs carbon dioxide and releases oxygen. When the physical and the mental converge, the energy of masculine and feminine unite. They come together in the divided inner self. The battle is over. The mandala is in the chakra and inside the chakra-mandala is the center, and inside the center is the true thing that does escape and is ever elusive. It is the god and the goddess, the way into and out of the center. This is like the mouth of creation that speaks the word and swallows it, too. It is the seed and the flower, the beginning and the end.

On my journey I would soon discover the ultimate destruction that we attribute to Mother Nature, which is death. On the surface it would seem that energy disappears and is gone forever, when death rearranges the physical body. This is far from the truth. Like the leaves and the animals that die in the depths of the forest or in the garden, the decomposition of their bodies renews the earth. Note the Buddhist sky burials and the funeral pyres of other traditions. Theirs is a more obvious connection to the continuance of energy from one form to another. Seen in a different light from the way we observe death in our culture, the body becomes an offering back to Mother Earth.

In regard to the experience of death I can only be grateful that some of my teachers were nuns. The acts of dying I observed would happen in the shelter of a spiritual space. My first patient at the end of my first year of nursing school was a sweet old man. He died the second week I was assigned to him. Despite being stunned and frightened, I was required to prepare his body for the morgue before his family arrived. He was a very old man but I had never been in the presence of death or known how quickly and permanently it takes hold.

Death, the corpse, sivasana, the wonder and terror of it, "a terrible beauty,"[7] the poet William Butler Yeats once wrote. All these events evoke questions about life after death, karma, the body remains in its descent into the bardo state, limbo, heaven, choirs of angels, hell, fire and the sleep from which we do not awaken. Or do we? Explanations and fears give way to dogmas in reaction to uncertainties. In youth all these observations and glimpses into eternity or any suspicions, therefore, about waking reality are tucked away for future examination. In a hospital setting all these unsettling thoughts are put aside while rigor mortis sets in, and we prepare a body for the family. In our society we value cleanliness and the sterile experience. We no longer prepare bodies at home or sew our own shroud, like my Orthodox Jewish friend, who was given permission to sew her own shroud; she was dying of cancer slowly and she wished to appreciate every moment of every stitch of her life. Normally there is someone else to do it. This is the time to say goodbye and we don't like that either. Ashes to ashes, dust to dirt, decomposition and the rapid return to our Great Mother are all to be avoided. Tenderly, reverently, we washed the old man's body, which had served him so well during his sojourn on earth.

When I finished washing his frail and lifeless body, I was sent down to the chapel to kneel and pray for his soul. If there is a good death experience, the quiet going-forth of a peaceful old man was the ideal preparation. After chapel I was asked to visit mother superior's office, where I was given a talk about the beatitudes and the avocation of nursing. I was still eighteen years old.

I would witness many death experiences in the next two years but one other stands out for a different reason. It was my last year, my last rotation, and I was assigned to the intensive care unit. A man in the prime of his life was wheeled into my care after a car accident. He was completely paralyzed and being fed through a tube. He was hooked up to monitors, and his beautiful spirit was completely conscious of his fate. Family members waited in an anteroom while he begged me to pull his life supports. "Please," he entreated, "no one will ever know." In the end I simply could not do it, and all these years later I wonder what happened to him.

I arrived in Africa for the first time in the late afternoon, as the sun began to set. The next day was my orientation to the hospital attached to the nursing school. During my tour, I had to step over dead bodies stretched out on the balcony corridors while my tour guide apologized for the cholera outbreak and promised to have the bodies removed by the time I started to teach. Down below us in the hospital courtyard fires burned and shrouded women ululated in the pitiful mourning of helpless despair. It looked like a scene from Dante's *Inferno*. The sound of ululating sent chills up my spine that resembled the awareness of kundalini. Death and awareness in combination was a powerful learning experience. Off the corridor were the rooms of the barely alive, for everyone knew that one came to the pestilence of a hospital as a last resort. One came to the hospital to meet death. Hearing the women mourning outside was a continual and cruel reminder of the possibility that life was nearly over. Resignation looked out of most faces. So what was the lesson?

On my toaster in the kitchen these many years later is a quote from Goethe. "Nothing is worth more than this day."[8] Nothing. Each morning I read this message with my coffee and toast. I savor these first bites of food and feel energy rise up my spine in gratitude for a new day.

Mother nature is a great teacher even when her lessons are harsh or cruel. The rewards of consciousness and the necessary struggle to separate our consciousness from the great and collective unconscious are like a list of must-haves for growth: heightened concentration, self-mastery, self-control, fearlessness and more portions of courage. Though this may sound like a betrayal of Divine Mother, there is nothing further from the truth. It is nearly every mother's greatest wish that her children find their own way to the best of their abilities and that they become who they were meant to become. It is a reflection on that mother that her contribution to creation was good and even beautiful. This is a mother's greatest reward. As for Mother Nature, she is confused and hurt right now, as only a mother can be who has been so taken for granted and unappreciated for her best efforts. This may sound too personified an explanation for some but only think of our own mothers and their feelings of abandonment and blame. This behavior by children is a sign of immaturity and a fear of separation. If too many material things have spoiled us and we have not had enough love, if these things were a misguided substitute for love, these are unfortunate circumstances. To spoil is to make rotten, as we all know, and it is not possible to spoil a child with love, only with things. These things have been manufactured and commandeered from the earth, in fact, stolen from Mother Nature. In our fear of separation and of the wrath of our Great Mother, we have tried to tame her, to use her, to manipulate her and to violate her. In return we want love from our children who will respond only by emulating us. Since we are all children, and we have all been mothers, only reflect on how we have gone about it for generation after generation.

True reverence for life, for the energy and the vision of the Great Mother, who is the womb of nature, is part of the daily devotions of millions of Islamic followers. The *fatiha,* recited each day, is a call to mercy and compassion. The poet Rumi once wrote of mercy as a virtue belonging to his feminine attributes, which are both terrible and tender:

> I am dust particles in sunlight.
> I am the round sun. To the bits of dust I say, Stay.
> To the sun, Keep moving.[9]

This beautiful poem refers to the fact that we are one with nature. The sun overhead and the sand beneath our feet are precious parts of us. Devotion and awe rather than violence are the true expressions of our gratitude and of our acknowledged faith in the continuation of life.

To understand that all the people of the earth are containers of great potential yet to be expressed, one has only to ponder the metaphor of the seed buried in the earth. There in the depths of the collective wisdom of ancestors who have gone before us and experienced all that they could before they departed, nothing is lost. Everything they struggled to know is gathered beneath our feet, a treasure to be opened. Its beauty haunts us. The enormity of that wisdom that has been won at a great price is ours to harvest. In the case of those African women on dusty roads, it is theirs to gather in compassion for their often-abused bodies and minds.

Our access to the energy of the Great Mother begins with an invocation in the first chakra. We know it through our instincts in the same way that the awesome energy of the whale absorbs and sends out sonar probes into the depths of darkness. We access this powerful energy by listening in the quiet of our hearts to the gentle rhythm of the earth and the still voice within. Then we know without fear, without a terror of our own knowing. When the caged bird is released, often it does not realize the cage door has been opened. It takes a few moments to regain equilibrium.

6

Negative Mothers:
The Dark Side of Mother

Out of chaos and darkness the light is born. In the unknown is where gnosis is made manifest. We have all been disobedient children and know that it is mother's task to put us back on the path and calm our fears. What we forget about dark shadows and silent sanctuaries is that they incubate our potential.

Inner consciousness and outer life, their connection and unity, have been under the microscope of scrutiny for as long as humankind has searched for wholeness. Intensity of focus within is accompanied by the image of light. An expansion of our lives in community can easily end up in a diffusion of this light. Sometimes it seems that our efforts can barely be seen. Knowing this, several years ago I made a pilgrimage to Tibet. What I sought was to imprint a mandala in the dust while I circumambulated Mt. Kailash, purported to be the most holy mountain on earth.

Holy Mt. Kailash is venerated by some of the major religions of the world such as Bon, Jain, Hindu and Buddhist. It is home to Siva, Parvati and their son Ganesh. Great historical personages such as Milarepa and countless pilgrims have circled it each year. In my mind I imagined this holy mountain from above the earth in a panoramic sky view. Below were the marks of my footprints on the path that circles the *axis mundi*. My circle took me from 15,000 feet to over 18,000 feet in elevation. For certain, organist Elizabeth Asklar would have said, "God can see us up here." We burned juniper incense at the highest elevation of our inscribed mandala, and we wrote on dozens of prayer flags the names of family and friends. Each day I walked with pure concentration on my breath. I focused on the beauty of this earth and on the light that surrounds us. At night I slept in the cold thin air with the stars within reach and my prayers became a part of my body. The moon was a blue moon in that month of May, making the month long Saga Dawa celebration most auspicious. All over the country pilgrims were on the move and prayers were being offered for the continuation of human kindness and for the freedom to pray in peace. In effect, my movement in a circle around the holy mountain was also a shift within myself. I have circled my inner self and can feel my boundaries within a miraculous vessel from which I live each day to my fullest.

But I was reminded, during my circling of the holiest of the holies, that there were those who circled the mountain in a counter clockwise direction. The followers of the ancient Bon religion, who are still numbered among one of the world's greatest religions, were there to create the same soul boundaries. They bring to mind the other side of the brain. Their actions remind me that that which does not quite make sense or fit with my worldview is seldom of any consequence. Their presence reminds me too, that I am not alone in the light. Surrounding me will always be an element of the unknown, an element that surpasses my understanding. I recall the lessons of the early Gnostics and how they existed in darkness until the light appeared. I welcome facts that challenge my own ideas of how light emanates throughout the world. The unknown is a part of my unconscious, so I try to remember that Divine Mother is a great and often inscrutable force of soothing darkness and creative chaos. She must be allowed to do her work in her own way. Part of my devotion involves my attempt to be courageous and to trust the dark forces that I cannot comprehend. I do so in the belief that out of chaos creations are born and reborn.

There is a shadowy aspect to the mother archetype. As part of the archetype, though the shadow is close to the surface of consciousness, it is, nevertheless, unconscious and virtually alive with a life of its own. It lays in wait until it is touched and awakened. There is no doubt that it is a powerful influence and a source of ancient wisdom. Often it is not ready to be touched directly. In myths and fairy tales these shadowy figures are often demon-like, in the form of the wolf, the old witch in the forest, the evil magician or the sorceress. Because these negative characteristics are by and large aspects of ourselves that we wish to deny or to attribute to others, often they are relegated to projections of those unpleasant qualities that we find objectionable about others.

Fortunately, aspects of ourselves can become positive projections. The one thing all projections have in common with one another is energy. Projections are carriers of repressed energy. Sometimes that energy is wasted in misdirected actions. We over or underestimate ourselves because our shadowy projections are not given their due. The demon simply may be an unacknowledged part of self that makes one uncomfortable, or it may be a truly demonic aspect that has grown and festered in a dark and secret life that has been hidden. We do, however, need to know our demons. We cannot project them all over the place and still remain eternally naive to our potential for good and evil.

There is a wonderful documentary film on the subject of projection and gnosis. It is in the library of the C. G. Jung Institute and contains interviews with three women who are Gnostics. Their stories reveal the meaning of dark projections. The first woman interviewed is June Singer, Jungian analytical psychologist and author of *Boundaries of the Soul*. Known for her clarity and erudition, Singer tells the tragic story of her daughter's death at age twenty-six. An only child, this young woman was on her honeymoon, when an oncoming vehicle hit her car. Singer's daughter's car crashed down a mountainside and her daughter died instantly. The viewer, who is told that Singer never understood darkness until the moment of her daughter's death, feels keenly Singer's grief and dark mourning. The next woman interviewed is Elaine Pagels, noted interpreter of Gnostic tests. She came to understand darkness and the Gnostic path after her young husband died in a mountain climbing accident, leaving her alone to care for their children.

However, it was the third woman interviewed who caught my attention and my heartstrings. Today, a Gnostic priestess in Palo Alto,

California, Rosalind Miller is a beautiful Cuban woman who had been a devout Catholic until the age of eighteen. One day, Castro's rebels carried her family away and imprisoned her. She knew nothing of politics at that time or during the time she spent in prison. She was tortured for years for no reason she could comprehend. On one occasion while being returned to her cell after her daily torture session, she was left to lie in a pile on the floor outside the commandant's office. She was expected to wait while her guard went in to chat with him. They laughed light-heartedly over a puppy inside the commandant's office that would be a gift that afternoon at his four-year-old daughter's birthday party. How strange, she thought, the man who gives orders for my torture has a four-year-old child and he loves her very much. As though nothing is amiss, today he will go to her party, laugh and give her this adorable surprise. Suddenly, she was filled with black hatred so profound she thought it might consume her. If an apparently normal man can do this, she thought, what might she do if given the opportunity to avenge herself? Then she knew that somewhere inside she, too, was capable of black and evil deeds. Suddenly, she was put on the same footing as her torturer. She never forgot what it felt like to see her own inner demon.

We are all connected at the deepest level of our unconscious and, whether we like it or not, one person's demonic actions stain everyone's conscience. In this collective stew we are all capable of horrific as well as great deeds.

What I must trust completely about chaos is its source. It lays somewhere deep inside of me, hidden and guarded, surrounded by dangerous avalanches and storms, earthquakes and volcanoes. Inside, I am naked and formless. I am vulnerable to injury and death but also exposed to my own redemption. There, the true mother I have always sought will embrace me with love. It is she who will hold me to her breast and protect me. Without her I am in the dark and I am afraid to be alone. There is a difference between her presence and her absence. I have come to discern that there is truly a great difference. Her absence creates the void whereby evil may enter. This is not a state of being I wish to explore.

How strangely we acculturate, yet think we are unaffected by the ancient past that has become a part of our present collective unconscious. Even the direction of my walk, whether to the right or to the left, has imposed an indelible imprint on my psyche. In ancient matriarchal societies no one would have thought twice about inscribing a circle backward. To the left is the feminine and therefore the Great Mother. This concept was manifest in the ways in which inheritances were endowed to children. Mothers turned over their powers to their daughters; they left their possessions to their daughters. The rulers were women and their names were passed to their daughters. Only mothers were considered worthy enough to know who their children were and only women were connected to the fertility of the earth. One could never be sure of one's father but mothers provided love and protection. Thus, sisters were more elevated in status than brothers, aunts over uncles and daughters over sons. Mother's reign encompassed death and mourning, earth and moon, night and good counsel. This was natural law, and the divisions that came with the lineage of men were unheard of in matriarchal cultures. Lineage was direct and visible and the separations of family groups unnecessary.[1] The term "beloved mother country"[2] was vaguely remembered in Greek memory to connote a very special relationship between mothers and children. They belonged together without a structural hierarchy of parentage.

Not until the Amazon warrior women of Greek legend did the matriarchy begin its conversion, slowly, toward patriarchal dominance. What began, apparently, as the elevation of love over defeat, eventually evolved into another cycle of domination. Succession turned from mother to father. Under the aegis of father's strength greater protection was sought. Women were elevated in status through marriage. They were given the reverence and honor that the matriarchal system did not promote. Eventually, strength and power evolved, at their lowest point, into domination, abuse and force. However, this is not the subject of this book. Certainly, it matters that women were demonized at the lowest ebb of this cycle. This demonization became the conventionally accepted reason to keep women in their place. Right became the right hand and the right side of the road. The right way and the wrong way to go about a complicated problem were associated with rational and/or irrational thoughts. The demonic appeared in the act of doing. Despite much talk of women's liberation, it is fairly obvious at what stage women presently exist in the larger swing of the matriarchal pendulum.

This is not to say that such huge cyclic endeavors as the dominance of men or of women happens consciously. To be immersed wholly in the mother is to be bound to the material earth with all its burdensome heaviness. Women in Africa or in the mud of rice paddies, for instance, can attest that women's subjection is not much fun. The imbalance of womanhood, epitomized by the Amazons who fought and won wars, administered their country, and did away with their male helpers was not ideal either. The Amazon women themselves tired of this extreme imbalance and wished to soften their warrior approach to life.

Male dominated women are covered in burkas and their bodies have been mutilated. They do not have the answers. Abused and subjugated women become angered and eventually find ways to avenge their humiliation on their oppressors. No one wins this power struggle. It is hard to depict what part of a cycle we are experiencing because negative and positive issues happen simultaneously. What may seem like an action undertaken for one purpose may, in the end, create its opposite effect. The demon is present in our lack of consciousness about what we do and our motives for those actions.

Jung speaks of the *temenos*. It is a safe haven from harm; it is the protective dome of grace. It may be equated with the dark center or cave and is a place of safety and healing. Within this protective space is the promise that conflict can be contained. Rest is possible. It is the description of the analytical hour. Courage is required to step inside the sacred *temenos*. Bravery is needed to see from inside this circle the unnecessary growth that surrounds us, to prune it and to cut at it with a sword of discrimination. Meister Eckhart, a mystical theologian, quoting Jesus, once said, "I come not upon earth to bring peace but a sword; to cut away all things, to part thee from brother, child, mother and friend, which are really thy foes. For verily thy comforts are thy foes."[3] Within the safety of the *temenos* many people have reached out to the world in a new direction with renewed energy.

The garden and the garden with a fountain in the center are evocative of churches, cloisters and homes that recall to our minds the protective *temenos*. The curved grace of these shelters evokes the mandala and the magic of mother until gently, we are coaxed in to confront our pain. Many a client of the analytical process has cried, "Why does this need to be dragged out again? Haven't I already cried enough?" But it is only in the protected cave that the bottom of the conflict is rescued from opposites and from further torment. It is only there that peace resides.

In the center of the circle or the square resides a deeply collective unconscious. This space opens to the wisdom of ancestors if one stands at its doorway with honest intentions. It is the voice of improvisation on center stage or in the Greek amphitheatre. It is the native talking circle, where one speaks only to the center of the circle It is the ritual dance, where ancestors make their wisdom known to the dancers through their feet on the earth and their receptive trance states. It becomes a terrible prison only when the words that are heard are unwanted, the tasks that are prescribed unwelcome. Now the dancer, the speaker and the actor recoil and deny what has been heard and said.

As a culture, we have placed sacred objects and events within the centers of our holy places. The *sanctum sanctorum* is the holiest of the holies; so we place the body and blood of Christ there. The Buddhist places himself in the moment, in that space between past and present, and waits in meditation. This practice is considered peaceful.

So where are the demon mothers in all this pacification? What is it that brings them raging and terrifying to our doorstep? When are the circles no longer magical or inviolable? Pausanias, the ancient traveler and geographer, wrote this report:

> There was in Athens a sacred precinct [a *temenos*] dedicated to Gaia and surnamed Olympia. Here the ground is torn open to the width of a cubit; and they say that the water flowed off here after the flood at the time of Deucalion; and every year they cast into the fissure wheatmeal kneaded with honey.[4]

When was the last time any of us offered the simple act of gratitude to Divine Mother? Sweet honey is the food of Divine Mother. Taken symbolically, it is appreciation for her abundance, her care and her love. When was the last time we offered really sweet prayers that do not ask for anything? When have we offered pure prayers, the devotion of our memories, of our love or of our attention? The chasm in the earth is her wrath; the water is the flow of her tears.

The mandala symbol, whether in the shape of a rose or of a cathedral, is used in yoga as a point of meditation. It is considered a spiritual tool to help focus the mind on a center. It wards off demons and concentrates our prayer and meditation. It focuses on that empty place in the center, the doorway to eternity and to the true self. The center is expressed by nothingness, yet is perceived as a rich space of four-sided wholeness. All is brought into a unified whole in this numinous symbol. Mandala symbols have been created spontaneously. They appear in the dreams or in the works of art of individuals who are on a quest for wholeness. The flower and the endless knot, the star and the cross, the swastika and the egg, the castle and the city, the all-knowing eye of God and the coiled snake, all erupt in dreams and paint themselves on canvas. However they appear, they are healing motifs. Whether they are made of sand or paint, of embroidery thread or of metal sculpture, they enhance healing. In Tibet the monastery town of Sanye is shaped as a mandala, the idea being that everyone who lives in Sanye lives from their center.

Since Greek times the *temenos* has been equated with the temple and used to demarcate the inner life from that which surrounds it. Traditionally, the temple was home to a god and to the rituals associated with that deity. With such delineation between inner and outer, between the precinct of the sacred and the outside world, the soul's personality would appear to be either a "prisoner or the protected inhabitant of the mandala [temple]."[5]

Traditionally, the deity was called upon from inside the temple. The question remains whether the church continues to fulfill its role as sanctuary. We know that exclusion and fear, intolerance and self-righteousness presently incubate within the walls of temples. We know that wars are incited from within many churches and mosques, and members of congregations become more like prisoners than free spirits. What, then, is the difference between a prisoner and a parishoner?

Jung took the concept of the *temenos* one step further, when he delineated the sign of the cross and the tips of that cross as a quaternity of characteristics that represents the personality. The popular personality test known as the enneagram was derived from Jung's original four types of personality. These types were: feeling, intuitive, sensate, and thinking types. Overlying this four-limbed cross was either the introvert or the extrovert function. The point here is that the shape of the cross, if filled in, would represent a square whose center is the center of the cross as well as of the *temenos*.

When I was a student at the C. G. Jung Institute in Kusnacht, Switzerland, Dr. David L. Miller was a guest speaker for an entire week of lectures. The topic is of no relevance to this story. What is relevant is the fact that I spent the first day unable to understand a thing he said. Normally very quiet in lectures, I raised my hand to ask for clarification. I could not understand his answer to my question. The next day and the next found me in similar perplexity with an added and growing confusion. It came to the point that a collective groan could be heard from the other students when my hand went up. On the fourth day I sat there too upset to raise my hand. When I saw Dr. Miller after class, I hardly knew how to begin. We decided to go for a glass of wine. After the third glass of wine we were both in turmoil. What had gone wrong with his lectures and my comprehension? On some level I realized the topic was not difficult, so what was the problem? We parted company with Dr. Miller determined to find a solution.

The next day was Friday and the last day of his lecture series. This class was attended by a large group of students as well as by the public and was held upstairs in a larger lecture hall. Dr. Miller commenced class by announcing that he wanted to try something different. I was in the second row, hoping expectantly that I would understand even a few gems of wisdom from a man whose lectures everyone seemed to love. We were to close our eyes during the lecture, he said, and listen through our hearts. Five minutes into the lecture my eyes sprang open and I stared directly into Dr. Miller's eyes. Yes, I understood every word. I am sure he summarized the previous four days of lectures for me that afternoon and I understood what he was saying.

The juncture of the body-cross in the very center of a four-cornered square also represents the heart. To hear through the heart is to understand. It turned out that Dr. Miller and I were two opposite personality types. We simply could not understand each other because we approached life's information from opposite directions.

The diamond of wisdom in the center of this tale is the function of the heart space or *temenos*. In that spot all the facets of my personal style combined with the facets of Miller's style of communication and what emerged was an understanding between us. As I tell this personal story, I wonder if the diplomats of this world could not come to the same place and whether in school our children could be taught this method of listening to each other. Such an approach to learning would change the world. Though I have never seen David Miller again, I know we will always be true friends of the heart. If we listen through the heart, is it possible to be imprisoned in ignorance?

Fear, especially fear of the unknown, is another word for demon. The demonic is a fact that we avoid and by our very avoidance we give it power. We have done this to the scapegoat whose existence is created by our own projection of fears. Most of us have taken out the wonderful children's book, *Where The Wild Things Are,* to read to our children as they reach the age when scary monsters lie in wait in the darkness beneath beds, or when bad dreams awaken a child. As grownups, we are not far from the reality that we describe as magical and illusory in children. How many of us are perfectly comfortable walking alone in the woods or on a city street at night, for example? But, as we notice in fairy tales, monsters have been known to be misunderstood. An entire entourage of princesses has kissed ugly frogs and monsters, which have awakened to find themselves turned into princes. Fear of marriage and of the unknown other has been a constant in history. Fears of death and loss, of pain and abandonment, compete to create demons. In other words, fears dissipate when we get close to them, make friends with them and come to understand why they became fears.

While Jung discussed the demons that possessed collective gatherings of cultures Europe was in the throes of a possession that first overtook most of Germany and Austria, and then the rest of Europe. In his often-read gem *The Undiscovered Self: The Dilemma of the Individual in Society*, he expressed his own concerns and fears as to what would happen to our civilization if our consciousness and the unconscious were not to become somewhat more connected. We cannot continue to walk in the abyss of unawareness and expect the psyche to overcome tragedy. We can be overtaken by the wrath of the mother in the form of irrational ideas and the actions that follow from them. It is irrational to put human beings in gas chambers; it is irrational to hold a young woman in prison for years and to subject her to torture daily; it is irrational to preach to thousands of churchgoers who feel superior to their neighbors and who exclude those neighbors from their daily lives. Without greater self-knowledge and exploration none of these acts will appear irrational to the ones perpetuating these attitudes and acts of cruelty. Without self-knowledge we are all susceptible to emotional coercion, whether it is at the irritating level of political correctness or in the real fear of individual action and subsequent political reaction. The distance between our thoughts and our actions is closer than we wish to believe.

What we value determines who we are. Our ideals, goals and purpose in life are what we cultivate through awareness. These cultivations pertain importantly to the mother archetype. How do we value, devalue or simply ignore what this means? Jung spent his entire life struggling to understand his anima. He claimed that "the more power man had over nature, the more his knowledge and skill went to his head, the deeper became his contempt for the merely natural and accidental, for that which is irrationally given—including the objective psyche, which is all that consciousness is not."[6] Today our hubris is so great we believe we can create global warming or global cooling, control hurricanes and the effects of floods, master mudslides and fires. There are many whose unease in the face of the negative mother is so strong they believe they are responsible for natural disasters. The reality, that we are just specks on the earth's surface, tolerated by nature, is too big and frightening a concept for us to absorb. It makes us feel insecure and little again, and definitely powerless.

Other manifestations of the demon in the unconscious realm of mother involve magicians, self-made saviors, incubi, witches, ghosts, devils and a demon inner child or two. Even these so-called evil entities have their opposites. Just as a magician can be seen as a savior, so the demon may turn out to be a daemon. Diotima once told Socrates that Eros was a great daemon.

Not only is Eros the lord of destruction, he is the death instinct. We would disappear from the face of the earth without his influence. Without our sex drive in the form of libido or sexuality we would be extinguished. Eros and his cherub image as Cupid epitomize love and romance but the other side of this archetypal figure is death. When unleashed before a naïve and unconscious person, the demonic goes unnoticed. This is especially true when the demon is unrecognized because it appears in an unfamiliar form. It can be overlooked because of habit or denial. One could say the demon might even camouflage himself as a normal man who appears to love his four-year-old daughter and comes bearing a puppy as a gift. The point of Diotima's conversation with Socrates was to acknowledge the two faces of Eros. As a daemon Eros is a catalyst for love and creativity in the form of the muse who may also wear a mask. The demon disguises itself as comfort in order to increase our inertia. We are surrounded by comforts in modern times. Our homes are heated, our meals gourmet, our beds thick and cushiony and our entertainments lavish. Spas and painless dentistry, cosmetic surgery and weight loss clinics are considered necessities. Our creature comforts come in myriad forms.

Throughout time, whenever the mother archetype has been undermined, the feminine has risen in revolt. Sometimes when this revolt occurs it looks like counter-espionage, and the Great Mother disappears beneath a cloak. Her hidden agenda resembles self-hatred and what her image mirrors is dissatisfaction. Since appearances are deceptive, one has only to ask what is behind this cosmetic mask and gaily painted façade. Where does discontent find roots? How does it grow big enough to initiate change unless it begins beneath the protective cover of self-deception?

This problem of projection has taken me a long time to understand. During my first semester as a student at the Jung Institute, it was necessary for me to find accommodation. This is quite an adventure in a foreign country while trying to save pennies for the long haul. My solution was a room in an apartment owned by an apparently lovely American woman who had married and become a Swiss resident years prior. The first of my experiential lessons in analytical psychology began that first month in the disguise of a loving mother who was a thwarted and frustrated woman. That semester I learned about projection, what it meant and what it looked like.

As soon as I had moved in to my room and found my way around school, my landlady began to be aloof and to avoid me. What had looked like a welcoming situation became distant and cool. Obstacles to the use of the kitchen and laundry became problems. Being friendly to the ten-year-old in the bedroom next to mine was frowned upon. Small talk stopped. So, I thought, I had misjudged the circumstances and would need to find a more amicable lodging in the future. What I did not find out until just before my departure at the end of the semester was that, some time before, my landlady had been rejected as a student at the school I attended. She came to demonize anyone who was a student there. I can only assume I was taken in as a lodger under false pretenses. Beneath the friendly exterior lurked her envy and her misplaced hatred.

On my last night in her lodgings, with my bags packed, laundry done and goodbyes said, I awoke at four in the morning, startled and shaking. Was I dreaming? What had awakened me? I tiptoed quietly into the hallway to use the bathroom. From there I heard mumbling and saw candlelight coming from around the corner in the living room. Assuming it was my landlady with her guest, a Nigerian woman to whom I had been introduced briefly the evening before, I entered the bathroom, turned on the light and froze. There on the sink was a voodoo doll with pins stuck all over it. I had become the object of this woman's misguided hatred for the institute that had rejected her. Instead of going back to sleep, I dressed quickly, left the apartment with my luggage and made my way down to the train station. I had only a short wait in the bracing morning air before the first train arrived and I was off to the airport. I put myself in the light by doing the Divine Light Invocation that I had learned from my spiritual mother Swami Radha and flew home that day. I felt that I had learned a great lesson about the unconscious, about the mask of projection and about the future perils that would confront me as an analyst. As I told Dr. Baker, I had much to be grateful for in being exposed to this phenomenon so early in my training. I will never forget that lesson. Yet I know that other incidents will appear in different and perhaps more subtle guises. My instinctual reaction to put myself in the light was a sure way to dispel the darkness. The demonic unconscious whose agenda was hidden had certainly been provoked.

The great and terrible mother is the negative side of the mother archetype. Most often the mother archetype is seen as the eternal vessel, the circle and the symbol of growth. The fact that presently our world is spinning rapidly in the arena of masculine consciousness means that the mother archetype has been relegated to the background. In that place she is slow and dark as well as unconscious and devouring. This is presently how mother, as unconscious and archetypal, is being perceived by the male world-view. Read this statement to mean that "the growing strength of the male corresponds to the increasing power of consciousness in human development."[7] While this statement is true, it is cause for fear. What is wrong with consciousness one might ask? Is it not to our collective and individual advantage to gain more awareness? Of course it is. The problem is imbalance. Consciousness that grows at the expense of the unconscious is not sustainable. Without knowledge of the depths, eventually awareness will sink back into a morass of blackness.

Creation, creativity and the arts are in trouble today. What comes first? How did contemporary art become cerebral and masculine? Why is it that administrative decisions are patriarchal? From where did disdain for the feminine influence in art originate? That is the current state of the arts, and it is artists who suffer from patriarchal domination. These statements may appear to be the nagging old complaint of women's liberation but I maintain that these issues really are about respect versus disregard for the mother archetype. When a male-driven economy can overwhelm a concert or an art exhibit with non-attendance, when television and video game absorption supersede opera productions and candlelight dinners, we have succumbed to masculine machines and to computer relationships. The mother archetype is struggling to breathe and is being snuffed out. Imbalance thrives.

What happens now? Artists starve, musicians resort to drugs, opera companies close their doors and American Idol takes front stage. We do not need to go to war to compete or to demonstrate hatred. Go backstage to see the seduction and the tears, the coercion and the suffering. These are our artists and their spirits are dying. No one truly cares about the formation of artists or the suffering of their mothers. The anxiety of artists has reached monumental proportions. It has not always been this way, despite what we are told. What we do not or cannot see is the vast and cyclical nature of the problem. Cycles like matriarchy and patriarchy are thousands of years coming and going. These observations are not made to blame or to judge our lack of knowledge. They are simply tiny corners of emerging awareness to be shared. In the sharing, may another soul awaken and then two and four, eight and sixteen.

What would it look like if the mothers became angry? What if their influence was askew and out of balance? Sharp-clawed harpies, lustful and cruel monsters, black nightmares, hungry destruction, devouring graves and the empty indifference of blood and war are some of her descriptors. Disease and continual sacrifice are all part of her kingdom. We can read about her influence in ancient myths and in daily newspapers. Despite the fact that we have experienced her wrath, we forget and we prefer to forget. Anything the great and positive mother can do, the dark and negative mother can undo. Hers is the abode of the vulture and of the grave. Her face is the grinning skull. Kali, Durga, Coatlicue, Amam, the Old Woman in the West and the Valkyries are a few of her manifestations.

When a negative mother complex occurs, there is cause to look for sickness and trauma. Trauma blocks the instincts from which this archetype otherwise springs whole and natural. In the world of psychopathology this disruption may look like the woman whose only goal in life is childbirth. She is the one whose self-diminution puts everyone and everything before herself. The marriage breaker or woman who must compete to be better than her own mother has a negative mother complex. We think of her as superwoman. According to C. G. Jung, these are empty women whose families may "impute to them anything [one] fancies", and they "please man enormously".[4] Everything is done in opposition to mother and on an inordinately unconscious level. The negative mother complex often creates the never-ending neurosis that takes years of effort to alleviate.

Perhaps it would be easier to understand her nature if we described more of her actions. She destroys words that help us to communicate; she burns us up in unending desire that we seem unable to control; she cuts at the heart, so that it may not be still but always agitated; she will not listen to any pleas; she causes weeping and suffering that will not stop; she hurts and slaughters for no apparent reason; she has a loud and harsh voice that causes fear and tremors; she ruins everything she touches and hides away to plot more and more of the same.

Fortunately, the negative side of the mother archetype is also the path to consciousness. Without her and the suffering she creates, we would not arise from our buried state. Pain is one of our greatest attention getters. Blessed are those who remember the past and learn from the mistakes therein. If our children are spared the great pendulum of too much and too little, they may not discover the path of consciousness.

The phenomenon called possession can be categorized alongside the demons. Simply stated, the mind-set of possession occurs when the demonic content of the possession is so unconscious that it overcomes the personality. Once considered the domain of Satanists, it is clear to us now that possession can affect entire populations, not just individuals. Enter the holocaust destruction of Hitler's Third Reich, the psychology of the crowd and even the counter-transference that can occur between analyst and analysand. Analytical psychologist Craig Stephenson does a thorough study of possession throughout the ages in his recent book, *Possession*. He emphasizes, particularly, the dissociation factor that occurs in trauma and the consequences one might expect from demonic possession while in this state. In the psychoanalytic hour the analyst is constantly acting like a bridge between the analysand's unconscious and consciousness in that *temenos* of protective exploration. The trick, on the part of the analyst, is to be aware of this process, for the unconscious is the dissociative end of the balance; it contains the repressed memory of trauma. In today's analytical practice we come across these contents frequently because currently trauma is under scrutiny in the analytic hour. Dissociation has become a focus of attention in neuropsychology, as well.

The issue here, in this reflective exploration of the mother archetype, is the necessity of acknowledging Divine Mother in the midst of psychic injury. Jung's comment, "When the god is not acknowledged"[8] applies equally to the goddess. Without a nod to the mother, the ego inflates and the analysand feels either all-powerful or out of control, as we see in Nietzsche's superman, Goethe's Faust, Hitler's motherland. "Evil spirits",[9] Jung called them, an expression still not accepted by the modern science of psychology.

Today the bridge that is so painstakingly built by the analytical psychologist in a process that takes months and years is also constructed in a process called Eye Movement Desensitization and Reprocessing (EMDR). Veterans returning from war, abused children and various other survivors of trauma can use eye movement sensitization awareness to build a natural bridge inside the brain. This process is used to connect left and right brain hemispheres and therefore both sides of an experience of trauma. We know that Jung's idea of right and left brain, or animus and anima, can be described differently by neurologists as functions of reason and emotion or rational and irrational ideation.

We now know that the brain severs its memory component during trauma in order that action may be taken to survive. Neurologically, in the treatment of trauma, a bridge is built between both sides of the brain to reestablish connections between traumatic memories and the perception of those memories. It is like uncovering a wound and re-circulating the life-giving blood so necessary to healing. However, as an analytical psychologist who also practices EMDR, I am aware of another center necessary to process the thoughts and emotions of the analysand. The center will not hold for psychologists if Divine Mother is not invoked to process these connections. Thus, the slower and more careful analytical method in which the analyst, through transference, walks beside the analysand is still valuable. Essentially, the third presence that walks beside them both is the healing mother.

Because it is the eye that seems to activate the re-connection process of one side of the brain to the other, it brings to mind the attributes of another chakra in the ancient kundalini yogic science. To this chakra is attributed control of the sense of sight. Strangely enough, this center or chakra is located in the gut where emotions collect and are purported to reside and churn. This ancient yogic knowledge was once under the divine aegis of mother. We have lost this ancient wisdom. In some cases it was destroyed deliberately. A recent example of such deliberate destruction is the college of traditional medicine in Tibet, which was destroyed by the Chinese. Truly, we are half in the light and half in the dark at all times. We are also changing continually.

We are miniature replicas of mother and father and we copy them. Where we are thwarted in our ambitions, we become unbalanced. We may even be caught in the negative domain of the mother, where we are denied what we want. Here are one person's reflections on these dark forces, as they claim her inner life:

> I get gratified by my rage at subverted ideals. I even hang
> onto what disappoints me to feed off the anger. The power
> of the rage is gripping. It may be fairly impotent outside,

but it fills me up, so I don't even notice that I don't really care about all those perfect standards and certainties. And I don't even notice that I'm being deflected from claiming my own life.[10]

One crisis resolves; another begins. Our dark and our light aspects change like the seasons, where the sun comes up and goes down at different times of the day, casting a new set of shadows around us. The crises of children are not the problems of adults. Our relationships with friends, family and gods change at different stages of life. Regardless of the changes, we remain two-sided and unique. How I may perceive the dark will be different from your perception. As we ponder the Great Mother or matriarchy, or the feminine, it comes to our attention that even opposites have their opposites. This division and sub-division can be seen as growth or as cancer, as good or as evil. These concepts, too, are seen through our own glasses and reveal just as much about the perceivers as they do about the perceived. Is it truly possible that the existence of a god can be good or bad, dark or light, evil or not? Our brains are two-sided, therefore the world as we will forever see it is two-sided. Chaos and paradox have more parts than two. Creation and destruction are beyond the comprehension of most humans. How then do we find solace?

As I circle Mount Kailash, I step lightly and breathe deeply. I become aware of the center of this great and holy mountain. It compels and it rejects. All around me are those who cry and suffer and cannot perform this sacred ritual. Seen from above the earth's surface, I can only imagine what Divine Mother sees. Felt from below, I can only imagine the weight of my personal burdens. I walk and pray, and I remember how my heart hears more clearly than my head or my feet or my arms. I imagine the cross that is the *axis mundi* and know it is my refuge and my strength.

My Tibetan guide offers me his hand and a smile. Two old Tibetan women pass by us and what, click their heels? How lightly they tread. We meet them again at the summit of the pass. They burn juniper incense and chant their lotus mantra that takes them directly to the heart of meditation. They have finished ninety-eight circumambulations of this holy mountain and will walk two more before they return to their village. Joy spreads from their eyes to their whispered prayers for peace. One hundred circumambulations or koras ensures them release from this round of earthly sorrows. I smile at them and place my palms together over my heart. "Namaste," we say to each other. May the highest in you be met by the highest in me. Somehow, I feel like they have shared some of the blessings of their devoted and sincere hearts with me.

Such solace and such blessings arrive through the least expected portals.

7

Mother of Dreams

Dreams are a vehicle of the unconscious, one of the few ways to access the wisdom of the ages from the realm of the Mother. She has collected every cell, gene and molecule of every ancestor who has ever lived, and she recycles this information during the night. One third of our daily allotment of hours is spent in sleep. Pay attention.

Dreams: what are they good for; why do we have them? One third of our lives is spent asleep and in the world of the dream. In effect, we spend one third of our time in the realm of the unconscious. For millennia, humankind has been fascinated with nightly forays into the soul of darkness. We use the expression "follow your dreams" when we think of inspiration. We refer to nightmares as those horses of the Great Mother that gallop at breakneck speed to frighten us until we waken. We try to catch elusive dreams because they are filled with such awesome events, and we wish to remember them forever. There are the big dreams and the mundane dreams, the vividly lucid dreams and the prophetic ones that can heal or destroy. Dreams are full of wisdom, the kind of wisdom that Jung referred to as collective. That means the accumulation of the wisdom of everyone who has ever lived and died on this earth. It is there, waiting in the dream world.

Some of us have heard of the dream of the scientist Friedrich Kukule who discovered the benzene ring because of his dream. His dream took the form of a snake biting its own tail. Thus we know that inventions frequently do come from dreams. Problems are solved and life's goals and paths are illuminated through dreams.

A life of impoverishment can be compensated for in dreams. Wishful thinking is how we often describe these dreams, and yet, if an individual can dream it, then it is in the realm of possibility in the unconscious of that individual. In other words, if you did this, this might follow; if you were like that, that might follow. Dreams do come true. It happens all the time. Possibilities are highlighted and brought to awareness, and from awareness much can occur.

Most people pay no attention to their dreams. Many clients laugh uncomfortably and tell me it must have been something they ate the night before. Yes, it could definitely be about what you ate. The body speaks through dreams. How else can it express itself unless it is through pain or nausea or congestion? The body and the dream world are of the realm of mother and the unconscious. Through them the body says, "Stop. You are allergic to this or that substance; you eat too much; you need to eat more; be kind to your body." Many a body dream that could have saved someone's life has occurred and been ignored. It was right there in a dream. Dreams have been ignored for so long in our culture that we no longer know how to hear them, to see them, to listen to their wisdom or to trust them. We have even lost the ability to interpret them or to catch them before they disappear.

The fact that our dreams have become elusive is a function of how much we pay attention to them and the credence we give them. Dreams have a life of their own; they belong to the larger collective unconscious and, as such, they do not need us. It is we who need them. If you pay no attention to their existence or do not believe in them, they will make no sense. In many cases they will not manifest or will stay beneath the surface of consciousness. Many of my clients do not remember any of their dreams until they begin analysis. Then they are astonished that dreams suddenly appear. When we choose to listen to them and to work with them, dreams come alive. I tell my clients to prepare for them, make space for them and always welcome them in their lives. If they work with me, they record their dreams in duplicate and then the work begins. So distant have our dreams become in our Western culture that we do not believe in their wisdom or in their healing.

Dreams have been demoted to entertainment and to queer responses to a bad meal. Is it any wonder that the Great Mother is somewhat put off by our attitude? Here we are given the gift of wisdom from her realm, and we sleep right through the night or maybe cannot sleep at all because we refuse to let our dreams intrude on our lives.

In ancient Greece the most profound healing was done under the aegis of Aesculepius, the legendary Greek god of medicine who used dreams as his voice. Underground, his handmaidens, the priestesses, prepared the seeker for sleep. There, on an altar, the sick or perplexed person who had come for healing was to sleep. Advice was given to prepare for the dream. The dream that occurred underground and under supervision was the cure. Afterward, it was up to the individual to go home and to follow the instructions received in the dream. If this sacred wisdom was ignored, the dreamer might live in fear of retribution from the mother of dreams. Wellness would never be achieved by anyone who ignored his or her dream. It is said that the dream came in the form of a snake, and the snake of wisdom took away the illness or the confusion. Sometimes sacrifice was required as recompense for bad deeds; action was necessary to remove the illness, and the form of action to be taken was made apparent through the dream.

Many people refuse to acknowledge the great importance of dreams because they are unwilling to change. We make excuses. The dreams are bizarre, unclear, ambiguous and impossible to follow. Mostly, we would rather scream, "I can't; I won't do it." This response comes down to a matter of trust in Divine Mother. Trust, or the lack of it, discussed in chapter one, hovers at the first chakra, along with the dreams themselves.

How, without trust in dream wisdom, could one possibly let one's self go into that unknown world?

As well as my private practice, where I see analysands, I work on a reservation of First Nations people. There, I am their trauma specialist and sometime dream catcher. To be entrusted with a dream by a native person, especially an elder, is to be honored indeed. Jung noted on his visit to the Pueblo people that natives still believed in the sacredness of the dream. Truly to believe in dreams is to follow the wisdom of the mother without question. Dreams, as honored by First Nations People, are accepted as messages from the Creator. No convoluted interpretation is needed because the dreams are quite clear and directive. They are not the complex mazes that non-native dreams have become. If a dream's direction truly is accepted, then it does not need to be couched in acceptable camouflage.

For instance, a man from another reservation came to see me. I did not have time to see him; I was booked and he did not have an appointment. I did not even get his name because I was persuaded to see him for just a few minutes. His young daughter had been killed under heinous circumstances. He was distraught, could not stop crying and spoke of revenge on the murderer. As we had only a short visit and he expected me to impart important wisdom, I asked him if he had had a dream since the child's death. Yes, she had appeared to him and asked him to hold her against his heart. Then he remembered that he had had the same dream while his wife was pregnant and again just before she was born. Knowing I would never see this man again because he had driven many miles for this visit, I told him he already had his answer from the Creator. "You are to hold your child to your heart until you hear otherwise from her spirit," I told him. She had never asked for anything from him except his love. We cried together and I reminded him that the dream had not mentioned revenge. Love was the answer. He was to hold the memory of her spirit in love for as long as it was possible to do so. He left fifteen minutes later, still in tears but with a healing heart. Now, he could mourn in a normal way. It would not be easy but he had his answer. The Creator had spoken through the dream and I felt reassured that he took the advice seriously.

Even lucid dreams of the daytime, what non-natives call hallucinations or delusional daydreams, are taken seriously by First Nations people. One old fellow with a diagnosis of possible schizophrenia came to see me. He was a delightful old man who was very lonely. All his friends and family were gone and he lived alone in a remote corner of a distant reserve. He began to tell me of visions he had each day from spirits of the dead. These were all friendly spirits of people he had once known. They told him things about the living, facts that were kept secret or taboo on the reserve. Finally, he asked me if I thought he was crazy. "No," I told him, "just lonely. These spirits come from the Creator to keep you company but, eventually, you must let them go." "You mean like on that TV show?" he asked in pretend innocence. "Yes, like the show on TV," I told him. I remarked that he must be very close to the Creator to have received such helpers. For what reason did he think they visited him, I asked. "They know I have things yet to do on this earth," he told me, "things I have not yet done. It is not time yet for me to join my friends and they know it." That was the last time I saw him. It was quite straightforward. Advice given from the spirit. Advice taken. Would that the rest of us could be on such intimate terms with our dreams. It is always an honor for me to be allowed to catch dreams, for this means I am in the immediate presence of the dream, along with my client who trusts me enough with such a treasure. It is a great honor. It is, in effect, a chance to be in the presence of the Great Mother.

Because all dreams come from the unconscious and the realm of the Great Mother, we may trust that they speak to us in ways that we can handle. The information revealed is always information we can deal with, if we so choose. As for nightmares, these are recurrences of an important theme that we have ignored. These are issues that we have overlooked or denied for some time and they demand immediate attention. A frightening dream tries to get your attention. It could be a dire warning: you are getting sick; you are losing your family; you are squandering your talents. It is beyond time to take action. We can never say we were not warned, and yet we pretend we did not know the wife would walk out, the husband had an affair, the kids were abused by the babysitter, the boss would not put up with one more tardy entrance or lost report. We already know and the Creator does not take kindly to bad behavior. We must not ignore messages from our dreams.

Sometimes I tell clients who have had the courage to write their dreams but not the courage to listen and to obey them, that they could go home and pray about it. Set the dream once again before the Creator and ask sincerely for a solution, maybe even a gradual step-by-step plan of action. There must be an action plan. Without a plan of action, eventually there will be stagnation and tragedy. We are not that far removed from the underground solutions of Aesculepius. Western man has always had to be threatened with disaster in order to straighten up. If you ask for the gift of healing and well being, and the gift is handed to you, you do not throw it out, misplace it or forget it. To ignore it is ignorance. To ask for a more generous gift is greed. To laugh at it and belittle the gift is a sign of hatred. These are direct insults to the mother of all dream catchers, the earth and her wisdom. In the Buddhist wheel of life these three actions of ignorance, greed and hatred constitute the hooks that will keep us trapped in the never-ending experience of sorrow. Beware.

Dreams and their study come mainly from India and China but also from aboriginal peoples around the world. The wisdom of dreams is not causal. It is irrational and therefore has little credence with conventional and scientific cause and effect. We live in an era of concrete rational thinking and frequently do not allow for the spirit to enter the soul. The writer Franz Kafka once commented that laughter and music do not need words. He could have added dreams to that comment.

The dream has its own language, the language of symbols and "archaic remnants".[1] These remnants derive from that collective unconscious, inherited from the old and instinctual experiences of the mind. This means that most often dreams are not personal. They draw on other wisdom that is ancient, culled from a library of human and animal patterns of behavior that we may have never experienced directly. The huge fund of knowledge that is ours each night is beyond our immediate comprehension. Jung called these archaic remnants archetypes or "primordial images".[2] They resemble patterns or imprints on our psyche, comparable to that of the goose, which returns year after year to the nest where it was born, or to the child who just knows how to suckle a breast. They allow the mother's heart to quicken when her child is injured.

So the language of dreams is rarely spoken but given to us in picture-form. Their language is expressed in colors and nuances, in associations and halos, in visions and in the inexplicable. Those who are closer to nature and to simplicity give thanks for such input. It enriches their lives and speaks of divine influences. Since we no longer believe in divine intervention, what we rely on must be controlled. We place our nightly revelations in categories and in their proper places. Perversely, we label these images as useless or as nonsense because we fear that they are signs of insanity.

Due to the fact that symbols are bridges to the unconscious and that the language of dream symbols is being ignored largely in today's world, those bridges are being neglected. Like anything left to a state of neglect, they are falling to ruin. When traumatic events occur in life and we need bridges to heal the dissociation that occurs between the two sides of the brain, we must rebuild them painstakingly. The point of rebuilding the bridges is to be able to cross over once again, to receive help in the form of understanding the trauma that we have endured and to accept the messages latent in the unconscious. That is how we can move forward, using what appears to be a most hateful experience to grow and to be who we were meant to be in this life. Without such action, the mind keeps the incident on an old tape that goes round and round on one side of the brain and never crosses over to the other side of the brain where consciousness resides.

Repetition does not mean that one can learn anything from an experience automatically. How many people do we know who repeat their story of woe to us over and over again? Old tapes of trauma go around on the same reel. Without bridges in the form of symbols we ignore dreams and enter a danger zone; for to disconnect from the unconscious is to lose touch with our instincts. Vivid and lucid dream images are not only memorable but they reinstate our helpful relationship with the valuable language of symbols and our connection with daily problem solving.

The dream symbol does not occur only in the dream. It may occur in the daydream and in the nightmare, in fantasy and in literature. Thoughts and actions that manifest in synchronization with inanimate objects and with unusual situations become important to the psyche. No one ever "invents a symbol"[3] or knows what it will reveal eventually. Religions, for instance, did not invent their symbols but merely awaited their revelations at a collective level and in their own time.

What is revealed through the dream is always something about the dreamer. No matter that the dream subject and symbol appear to be about the neighbor, the cat, the street or the inside of a house, it is still about the dreamer. Themes often recur and shift shape to let us see the problem differently. It is a kind and gentle way that the psyche has of subtly and subliminally shining a flashlight around the dream chamber. It is a wise way to expose different facets of an issue. We prepare ourselves for what we can accept and we expand that vision as we gather the flickering shadows. Plato once remarked on the cave shadows as the only true experience that man understands. Otherwise, we are staring into the light, and it is blinding; it is too much for us to deal with light directly. We must study the shadow rather than the direct and blinding light. Another way to express this is to say that one cannot look upon the face of God and continue to live as before.

Not everyone has the courage to work with his or her dreams. I am only grateful that my exposure to my own dreams was done gently and slowly. First, there was the work at Yasodhara Ashram where Swami Radha's dream method and Carl Jung's method of dream analysis matched perfectly. While the emphasis at the ashram was the spiritual dimension of those interpretations, the Jungian interpretations were first psychological and then spiritual. My first exposure was inspirational. I went home and was invited to join a dream group. We met weekly for ten years. Ideals, meaning of life, purpose and goals for self-realization: these became the focus of my dreams and of my actions. This may sound like a backward way of going about a quest for self-discovery, but it worked and it felt safe. We are told that we never receive a dream message that we cannot handle. So take courage.

I discovered that the main theme of my dreams for years had been escape. I had to escape from mother's wrath and envy at a young age. In my first recurring dream of escape, I was six and running from a huge female lion. A second dream of escape was from home in which an apocalyptic four horsemen had been hiding. To escape I had to reach grandmother's attic. In this escape motif I was almost captured, but I moved on. Finally, as a teenager, I began to put my escape plan into action: first, the tobacco fields to earn money, then away to school, then to Africa as a teacher. Suddenly, fate took the theme out of my hands and I was immigrating to a new country far from home, with a young husband. New life, new country, new baby, and new landscape; suddenly I felt disoriented and lonely, very lonely. In my dreams I had become a wanderer. Then I met Swami Radha.

The escape pattern began to manifest consciously until I discovered that each time I realized I was running or escaping from a circumstance, a person, a fear or any other emotion, my lesson was completed, over, finished. I came to realize, however, that one aspect of understanding leads to another. Finally, it becomes more of an adventure than a terrifying fear. I began to wonder when the escape theme would reappear again. I began to watch for it in various corners of my life. The escape theme, in effect, became my friend. These days, when occasionally it still appears, I know that I have an opportunity to grow. Inevitably, I feel a thrill of anticipation. I wonder about the form my adventure will take.

In my late teens I started to dream of Africa until, at last, I was there in reality. It was there I met my husband and it was there that I began to observe other women. In their movements I knew there was more than I could fathom. It was not until I gave birth to my own daughter that the dark African women with their walk of acceptance came into my dreams. Archetypes produce healing.

To follow a dream one needs to perceive the setting and the direction in which the dream points. Obviously, each of us is oriented differently and thus we perceive directions differently. Ingeniously, we will interpret the dream in our own way. When Jung was about to categorize personality types, he made this observation:

> I was always impressed by the fact that there are surprisingly many individuals who never use their minds if they can avoid it, and yet they are not stupid, and an equal number who obviously do use their minds but in an amazingly stupid way. I was also surprised to find many intelligent and wide-awake people who lived (as far as one could make out) as if they had never learned to use their sense organs. They did not see the things before their eyes, hear the words sounding in their ears, notice the things they touched or tasted, and lived without being aware of their own bodies. There were others who seemed to live in a most curious condition of consciousness, as if the state they had arrived at today were final, with no change in sight, or as if the world and the psyche were static and would remain so forever. They seemed devoid of all imagination, and entirely and exclusively dependent on sense perception. Changes and possibilities did not exist in their world, and in their 'today' there was no real 'tomorrow'. The future was just the repetition of the past.[4]

Thus, whether we are introverted or extroverted and whether our first personality style is intuitive or thinking, feeling or sensate, we must find a way to put our dreams into action. Jung's description, while accurate, does not take into consideration our desire to learn and to overcome the limitations of a single functional way of being. Our ability to change and grow by listening to our dreams can never be underestimated.

A Middle Eastern man brought his son to see me. The father was very demanding, angry and shouting. He told me he had just seen five other therapists. Each had been given one hour to fix his sixteen-year-old son. I, too, would have exactly one hour, during which father refused to leave the room. It was immediately apparent that the son was intimidated by his extroverted father and not of the same personality type. So I asked the father questions about his own life while I let his son listen. When the hour was over, the father conceded that the session had been beneficial and that his son would be back. However, what I soon discovered from the son, when he was left alone with me, was that his dream of the future was to become a film artist. He wanted to document his world but was afraid of his father's reaction. He was right to intuit his father's fear for him. It was the immigrant's fear for a child in a newly adopted land. What I uncovered in their family history, however, was poetry. Apparently, the father's grandfather had once been a poet in their home village and was revered immensely. The father had more pride than fear, it turned out, when he heard what his son dreamed of accomplishing. I had to change the clinic diagnosis from depression to oppression and hope that the father would continue to loosen his stranglehold on his beloved son.

Fortunately, I am extroverted with a feeling function, while in this second half of my life I have become more introverted, with intuitive inclinations. Otherwise, neither father nor son would have accepted my interpretation of the dream messages that emerged. It is always best to learn whether any one dream interpretation resonates with the dreamer. Compatible personality types resonate with the same dream interpretation. What may feel like prejudice or intolerance may be simply a miscommunication based on incompatible personality types. It is, after all, the dreamer's dream. When there is no recognition of the dream symbol, there is no resonance to the dream message.

One of my most traumatized clients had once been in a life-death struggle. This dangerous encounter was followed by a year in hospital while he was treated for nearly fatal wounds. He was still in a lot of pain but his family responsibilities were greater than ever. He dreamed that he was being chased up a hill by a pack of wolves. Gasping for breath and nearly dead, he spied his vision animal as it came out of the forest to fight off the wolves. During one of his surgeries, this man's heart stopped, and he was declared officially dead for several minutes. Then his heart started spontaneously, and he returned to life. I interpreted this dream as his having a strong and courageous heart. This interpretation instantly spoke to him. He left the session a bit taller and more able to cope with his many real struggles. Of course, there were the wolves following him; his survival instinct told him to run and leave it all behind. However, since his responsibilities now included children to raise, it seemed that his heart would prove up to the fight. It is also possible that he has been chosen by the fates to become a healer, eventually, for that is another meaning of the heart that has healed itself. He must discover this possibility on his own; it is only my private interpretation.

As a catcher of dreams, I am always reminded of the Dalai Lama, who often repeats that we are all searching for happiness. If this is true, and I cannot but believe that it is, then the unconscious that is submerged in darkness is always seeking the light. Dreams are a ray of light that shines through the darkness. Dreams belong to the domain of the Great Mother and they carry enlightenment from her realm of the forgotten.

Because the symbol always expands in meaning to express more than we can imagine consciously, the symbol may become numinous or holy. That is, the symbol is capable of transcending ordinary experience, capable of expanding awareness to levels previously unknown.

Despite our limitations, we are capable of catching glimpses or facets of that refracted light of understanding. It is like the prism my grandmother left me when she moved out. There it sat in the freezing cold winter sun and beneath the glaring humid heat of summer, a constant reminder that the world is full of hidden colors. Crystal colors flitted along the sun porch that was my own little bedroom, and on the saddest of days, purples and oranges, pinks and blues landed on my hands or on my clothes and comforted me. Even today, the most powerful prayer I know is the Divine Light Invocation taught to me by Swami Sivananda Radha.[5] It goes like this: "I am created by Divine Light; I am sustained by Divine Light; I am protected by Divine Light; I am surrounded by Divine Light; I am ever growing into Divine Light." To be protected and sustained by light, surrounded and birthed each night in light, is a true blessing.

Why do we seek symbols and rejoice when we dream? We see a kaleidoscope and a chaotic jumble of images, and they inspire us to be on the lookout for more. Our nighttimes are cathedrals.

Namkhai Norbu describes the Dzogchen practice of dream awareness and the meditation that follows. In his descriptions of this Tibetan practice, clarity and guidance through dream work manifest as light and as a greater knowledge of our purpose. Through a vigilant alertness dreams present themselves for inspection. The dreamer may attain a state of self-realization through this spiritual tool. Potential is uncovered, knowledge and wisdom attained, and illusion seen through. The heart is engaged.

Buddhists claim that through this dream practice of attending to light the karma of past lives may be burned off. Once this happens the body will be energized and require less sleep. This practice is not to be mistaken for lucid dreaming. Instead, it is described in tantra as "the moment in which one meets the mother light."[6] How beautiful to fall asleep in the arms of Divine Mother with an image of light, there, in the place of the third eye, the place of inner sight.

Healing occurs through dreams. The renowned sleep clairvoyant Edgar Cayce maintained that the mind and the soul live in the body. He deduced that dreams often refer to the body's state of health. Whether it is a dream that deals with constipation, circulation or complications of major surgery, it is nevertheless evolution that is depicted in dreams and guided by the Great Mother. Matter and creation, in Cayce's view, could not be ignored or separated. As matter the body awareness we manifest is all part of our health and welfare. Every night we have the opportunity to be in touch with creation. Without this attention to creation growth ceases and death soon ensues. To dream of the body is only one level of the dream but the most basic and certainly, the most essential. Again, it is a common joke that a bad dream happened because just before bedtime the dreamer ate something that did not agree with him or her. On one dream level this is true and because the psyche of soul is part of the body, good mental health is equally effective in the treatment of the body. Body attitudes, for instance, are often symbols for a psychological attitude.

Before his death Jung maintained that psyche and body were energy forms that changed over time. What held the body's energy mass intact was the intensity of the psyche's energy. He was quite attuned to the ideas emerging in physics at that time and this theory coincided with modern physics and its approach to form and matter. Physical matter, which includes the body, is subject to time and space and so death is explained as a de-intensification of energy. This means that the psyche and the soul fade slowly away, leaving the rest of an old body behind. Dreams that occur before death often have concurred with this energy theory. Light becomes the focus of such dreams. Jung gave examples of dreams that explain the manner in which we take our leave of Mother Earth. He quoted a patient as saying, "The whole thing [the dream] was like a transformer, an energy transformer, which transported me into a formlessness beyond time and space."[7]

The fact that, in our Western civilization, we have normally buried the bodies of the dead does not preclude the fact that others choose sky burials and various types of air borne rituals to send the body-soul on its way. Perhaps it is because the Eastern view tends to combine body and soul. By releasing the body what results is the state whereby the soul is also released. In the West we have separated the body and isolated it from the mind or the soul, so it is no surprise that we bury the corpse in order to allow the soul access to heaven. The Catholic Church has gone so far as to state that, unless the soul has conformed to certain church rules, the sanctuary of a church burial in a church cemetery will not be allowed. This infers, of course, that the soul is inordinately sullied by the body and actually might be contaminated, so access to sacred burial is denied.

A most important work on the dreams of the dying is *The Death of a Woman* by analytical psychologist Jane Hollister Wheelright. It is the documentation of a woman's dreams and her struggles while she is dying of cancer. She was only thirty-seven years old. "Sometimes I dream of a white boat gliding across the water. It's death coming for me. I want to get on that boat and at the same time I don't want to".[8] This was her first dream in analysis. By the last month of her life this young woman was able to stay closer to her unconscious with less fear. Wheelright writes, "Her last dream, along with evidence in earlier dreams, suggested that she had achieved a kind of full circle, a summing up. It is my hope that having finally accomplished the task laid out for her in her first dream and again in her dream of God, she returned peacefully, as the mother goddess, to unconscious ongoing life."[9] The courage to look at her dreams while in the process of dying took this young woman through and beyond time and made of her life something extraordinary. It would almost appear that the most important purpose of her life was to look at death without fear, without resentment, without regret and, at last, to accept the embrace of the Great Mother.

Maria-Louise von Franz, a student of C. G. Jung, once had a conversation with a dying woman that was also about transformation. The woman told her:

> This is a very beautiful feeling, on the one hand, but also a very strange one. One time runs, the other stands still. And I can even influence it myself—a little bit anyway. One feeling is quite far away and deep *as if I could be everywhere at the same time.* So I feel as if my body were somehow like air, or rather like light—as if there were no limits . . . . The other feeling is as if someone wants my moments. This goes on and on. I can't stop it. It is as if I am becoming less and less.[10]

From substantial body to disappearing light, the transformation to death takes place as energy departs from one form of existence to perhaps another. In this process whatever level of consciousness we may have had fades into the unconscious.

Sometimes the transformation we undergo takes the form of acceptance. Acceptance is the antithesis of fear and resignation. Simple acceptance is the antidote for fear in everything we do. This was the message from my dreams that took so long for me to understand. For years I wondered what those African women had to do with me. Self-acceptance is hard come by without a mother's hips to keep time with the pulse of the heartbeat of the world. Somehow these women understood that birth is a tragic event and life short, very short in many countries. So they held their children from morning till night; they fed them from their breasts; and they sang oftentimes to a rhythm that was in keeping with what they heard from mother earth. Their dusty walk was like a public apology for the materialism of the world. They counted on only the essentials, and only love survived fear.

I sit here and remember my dreams of the black women in the African desert, walking along those dusty roads with their children on their hips. I hear the ululating in the hospital compound or around the fire at night. Body and soul come together in their cries, which are profoundly close to their ancestors and to the ground. For them death is a new birth. And birth is instantly death.

In our society today there is not enough preparation for death. We do not acknowledge that death will provide for new life. We tend to avoid death. Thus, we often observe the vague human mind that sits, slouched in a wheelchair, unconscious of the future, without realizing how close it is to the act of transformation. Everywhere mysteries exist. The dream that could reach into the future goes unrealized.

Some of us have had the experience of hearing voices in our dreams. Once this happens we realize that other lives await birth and their own chance to evolve or self-realize, and we never forget those otherworldly voices. For instance, soon after my analyst Dr. Ian Baker died, he appeared in my dream, telling me to "write, rite, right". The next day I received the phone call informing me of his death.

In many cultures the dream was an opportunity for a messenger of God to appear. Known as the garuda bird, the winged angelic being, the dove of the Holy Spirit or simply the messenger-guide, the dream is a channel for communications with the unconscious. "In Euripides we find another interesting aspect of dreams when he calls lady earth 'Mother-of-black-winged Dreams.'"[11] He describes the sleep and the dream as that state that occurs when "the soul is freed from its tomb (the body). Whereby it is sensitized and so able to perceive and converse with higher beings, a thought that was also held by the Pythagoreans."[12] As I mentioned before, dreams in the underground realm of Aesculepius were attributed to a fount of wisdom. They were granted high significance and reverence. Such dreams were treated with the greatest respect.

The ancient Greeks, from Aesculepius, whose followers sought the underground incubation period where dreams manifested the advice of gods, to Plato and Aristotle, who classified dreams as precognitive and prophetic, believed that through dreams the divine somehow spoke to the dreamer. Daydreams were important because the telepathic atoms of the psyche were transmitted at that time and the soul traveled to reach farther than it would in the waking state. To the Greeks the dream world was one to be studied, documented and taken seriously. Medical diagnosis, creativity, wellbeing and health, sacrifice and the building of great temples, were predicated upon dream interpretation. Those who were particularly talented in the work of dream interpretation were considered graced by the gods and were often endowed with a certain enthusiasm for life. In general, work with dreams was honored and, perhaps because of this high regard for the content of dreams, divine elements often appeared as dream visions of great worth.

Maria Louise von Franz was a dream expert in her own right and eventually one of C. G. Jung's most devoted assistants. She wrote extensively of dream content. The nightmare particularly interested her because of its urgent message and its repeated nature. The persistence of the nightmare speaks to the psyche and demands recognition. It presents solutions to problems and responses to the world of the mother. Von Franz referred to this world as demonic, devouring and cruel. It is nature personified. Nature's world manifests as terrifying and emotionally draining. Vampires, blood-sucking murderers, dangerous women and evil ghosts inhabit this region. For men who step into this realm of mother, it is an indication that they have not yet completed the work of separation from mother. In our culture mother has gone underground and retaliates. In reality she draws away life energy through the dream world until the daytime is described as listless and grey. In men's dreams she may look like a beautiful and alluring woman, while being someone the dreamer needs to fear.

For the woman who has not separated from her father, demons appear. Their curse is that she is not good enough and never will be good enough. She feels she is being watched but often her limbs are missing. What can she do? She is helpless, faceless, cannot find herself. It is no wonder that so many women feel the need for lots of makeup or that they feel or act as though they are overly special without apparently valid reasons. They are trying to hide from father's judgment.

"Jung called the male personification of the unconscious in a woman's dreams the 'animus' that is the Latin word for spirit".[13] It is the counterpoint to the male dreams in which the female personification of his unconscious is called the 'anima'. Anima is the Latin word for soul. For the woman, the animus may appear as the strong man, the hero or, conversely, if the animus is inflated, a rabid animal, a hanged man or a man who is brutal and cold. The animus separates a woman from her own energy. This is currently the experience of Middle Eastern women behind their veils. Tyrants dominate them and, in turn, their inner and relentless father image dominates their own sons. In an unconscious cycle the women who are victimized make victims of their own children. The cold and critical father can never be appeased. Sylvia Plath wrote extensively in her poetry of this relationship with the negative father who overshadows the mother anima. The poem "Daddy" describes him:

> You stand at the blackboard, daddy,
> In the picture I have of you
> A cleft in your chin, instead of your foot
> But no less a devil for that . . . [14]

Women who are overcome by their fathers cannot keep their feet on the ground. They are imprisoned and weightless. They feel they need weapons and they judge themselves harshly. What they really need is to make friends with their dreams, take on the reflective attitude that returns balance, listen to the voice of instinct and tend to a spiritual dimension of energy. The way to do this is through greater attention to dreams. Like living entities, dreams respond to a respectful and willing approach. They must be taken seriously. In return they put us in touch with consciousness in the form of self-knowledge, purpose and the meaning of life. They become our friends to help us grow in an atmosphere of intimacy and understanding.

In our busy world the connection between a dream and waking life is tenuous. Those still close to nature connect directly to their dreams in a more clear way. Recently, a pregnant woman of the First Nation told me of a dream of her miscarriage. In the dream she was carrying her aborted fetus close to her heart. Later, there was a ceremony among the grandmothers for this little miscarried child. They blessed it, showed it to the mother and reminded her to keep this child's spirit close to her heart. In effect, the ritual reinforced the dream and, as she said, "Now I will never forget this little one. It will never be alone."

Through dreams we perceive what we must do to keep us happy and well. Like intuition or a sixth sense, we develop the ability to know what to do next. We learn how to be in the world and how to heal ourselves. Small revelations happen on a daily basis through dreams but this only happens if we trust what we see. To dismiss a dream as 'just a dream' is to miss out on an opportunity.

Poets never dismiss their dreams. Through them comes a different world-view; a new color is added to life's palette. In earlier cultures big dreams and those that repeated themselves were told to the community so the community might act on the dreams. "That is why in antiquity and in the Middle Ages dreams were held in great esteem. It was felt that they expressed a collective human truth."[15] This fact is often comforting in the case of big dreams that are archetypal or scary in content. To know that one is not alone in suffering or in joy is the essence of humanity.

In this respect the aspect of dreams that appears to unite opposites is unique. The concept of paradox, where two opposites retain their position until a third option appears to unite these contradictory positions, is a unique function of the dream. The contents of the opposite positions come together in the night. The two sides mix in a surprising way to create a resolution that had not been considered previously. The dream is amazingly creative. Invention as well as peace and harmony owe much to the dream.

James Hillman and Margot McLean have produced a magical book called *Dream Animals.* Hillman, whose background derives from the work of C. G. Jung, and McLean, a visual artist, collaborated on a portrayal of the appearance of animals in dreams. In a unique and creative approach to the study of dreams, we find ourselves, as readers, in the atmosphere of instinctual behavior. McLean's artwork puts us there in a misty and undefined world so remote in time and landscape that momentarily we are lost. This, as Hillman would point out, is exactly the world of the archetype. There, the questions we need to ask the animals are vague and indistinct. We have learned much from the appearance and behavior of animals but have we ever known them? McLean implies that the knowing we once had was lost. I wonder if we ever knew these creatures. Only through dreams do we come closer to their natures. Only through dreams do we make connections to our own behaviors that resemble the animals. The cat, the dog, the snake, the frog or the crane: only through the dream that delves into our body cells do we learn that we breathe the same air, touch the same space and fear the same fire.

Animal archetypes are explored through the body in certain yoga asanas but, usually, unless it is through the method described in *The Hidden Language of Hatha Yoga*, the body's awareness is kept in the body. Through animal dreams the animals connect us to an ancient archetypal wisdom that reminds us of our nearly lost instincts. What to fear, what to flee, of what do we need to be suspicious? In other words, our defense mechanisms have been learned directly or indirectly by our observations of animals. Their appearance in our dreams gives us pause. In the Hidden Language yoga method, asanas or poses are done in a reflective and conscious manner, and the images and body observations that occur are honest reflections. They are messages of the stored wisdom of the dream-body.

Animals make us pause because their way of being has been one of adaptation to their environment—to Mother Earth. Right now, we could learn from this realm. Our disconnection from a true awareness of nature is profound. Sports in the outdoors, competition, exotic nature resorts where we watch animals through a protective window: these are poor substitutes for intimacy with Mother Nature. It would be better for us to stand in the water at the edge of a flowing stream, to feel river stones beneath our feet, to watch the birds and the bugs, to follow the fish, to absorb the air and the sun through our skin, to get wet and sing like the stream. This is what every wild animal on earth does each day. When animals come to the stream there is a truce. They know that water is essential to life. By the stream they co-exist peacefully and tolerantly.

One of my clients, a pregnant woman of the First Nations, related her dream. Attached to the dream was a sense of fascination that could not be dismissed. She dreamed that she would have a green frog child and that the eyes of this little person would be placed differently from those of an ordinary child, differently from an ordinary frog, as well. Our conclusion was that this child would see life differently, perhaps in a unique way, for the frog is a vital symbol of many aboriginal people. It lives on the leaves and herbs of medicinal plants. It is close to the wisdom of healing. For years this young woman had sensed that she, herself, would be a medicine woman some day. This child was the symbol of a new beginning under the teachings of the frog. The frog's innate wisdom would be instructive to both her and her child. The rightness of the dream interpretation vibrated in the room. Excitement and hope filled the air. In years to come I will follow her growth and that of her newborn child.

In her work, *The Inner Child in Dreams* Kathrin Asper explores the dreams of childhood and of the child within each of us. To begin, the image of a child, any child, is itself a symbolic motif in dreams, one that is archetypal. It points to the past and to the future to show us how we have lived our lives and the possibilities that still exist. The mother-child bond is synonymous with these images because children do not grow without a mother caretaker. To survive, to grow, to experience the world around us means mother is present. Of course, the positive aspects of children are most often depicted in child-like images: innocence, happiness, holiness, growth and delight. Yet, "the history of childhood is one long horror story in which abuse, abandonment, intentional starvation, murder, neglect, atrocious swaddling practices, and educational methods harmful to both body and soul were legion. Only rarely are other ways of dealing with children found in history."[16] Reality forms a sharp contrast to the symbolic meaning of the child. The future and hope reside in the symbolic children of dreams.

However, every symbol has two sides. The archetype is held together by opposites. For most individuals the reality of what was and the possibility of what can be is the focus of therapy. Accurately or inaccurately, the focus on mother is often unclear. Not much is remembered consciously about one's self in early years. Mother is more often remembered through events that included her. The child image that appears in a dream, whether that child is recognized as part of the childhood of the dreamer or not, nevertheless, represents the dreamer.

Mothers have a hard time with this fact. Often their dreams are images of their children, and it is not easy for them to separate their own personality traits from those of their children or their own dreams from those of their children's concerns. Take for example the young native woman who dreamed of her future baby as a symbol of healing medicine. Her dream contains the possibility that this young mother may become a medicine woman some day. On the other hand, it is entirely possible that her dream may have been transmitted to her unborn child. It is quite possible that both mother and child have the same healing capabilities.

Shamans have been born into this family in past generations. The dream was clearly about potential in the future.

We are all guilty of promoting the one-sidedness of the child archetype. We look back to our own childhoods and remember selectively. We did not know the circumstances of life for our parents, their own inner children or their day-to-day struggles. Rare is the child who perceives these other-generational facts. Childhood is egocentric, as it must be for the child to grow. Other influences need to seep into this little and open book that is the real child. Unfortunately or otherwise, children are often the repositories for a parent's unfulfilled life. I do not say this to infuse parents with guilt. It is a simple fact. Perhaps this is the way evolution occurs. Children inherit any left over work not finished by parents and then, consciously or unconsciously, take up the challenge. While some people resent this fact others grasp the challenge in both hands and take on the task willingly. Dreams help us to recognize possibility. Children often dream of greatness.

The sins of the fathers, it is said, are carried for generations. The sins of the mothers are equally powerful. Of course, parents who have worked through their own dreams from childhood leave their children more space to deal with their own dreams. Any business inherited from parents will manifest as confusion. We all have heard small children calling one another names, insulting and blaming one another for situations about which they know nothing. Yet when children blame their parents, they are partially right to do so because it is their parents who have been unconscious channels of denial. It is their parents who have passed on to them the problems and prejudices that their own psyches have not resolved.

It is easy to see this concern in the First Nations people who live mostly on reservations. Many grandparents were victims of residential school trauma. Later they were sent back to the reservations to pick up the pieces of their lives in isolation. They, in turn, sent some of their children to residential schools or treated their children as they themselves had been treated. Now there are beautiful grandchildren trying to cope with the world, who are completely confused about their inner feeling of despair and sadness. They cannot possibly understand that they have inherited the sadness of their elders. Despite their love and honor for the elders they cannot know that they carry their burdens for them, now two generations later. Many are drug addicts rather than alcoholics like their parents. And those who have tried so hard to be conscious cannot find spouses who are like-minded.

Nevertheless, my dreams are still my own. Despite the heavy burdens of past generations that some people of the world refer to as karma, and despite all the baggage we bring with us, we are required to take responsibility for our dream's message. Parents and grandparents make mistakes. Inevitably we, too, will make mistakes. Sometimes all we can do is acknowledge the past, mourn for those mistakes, then carry on with new determination. We look to dreams for an examination or analysis of our sources of rage, intimidation, frustration and depression. Through dreams we develop self-compassion or we direct love and compassion to the right channels. In fairness to ourselves we are asked to take responsibility only for our own actions and attitudes, but first we must understand what these are. In dreams parents represent masculine and feminine issues in the archetypal realm; they represent the universal implications of their archetype; they also reflect the very personal and individual level of interpretation of the facts of everyday life in the dreamer's world.

With an increase in the problem of depression in this century we try to understand its cause. To depress is to press down, burden and overburden the psyche with negativity and hopelessness. Life becomes gray and meaningless. Guilt and even shame are inexcusably passed on to the small child. Secrets are kept. Until there is a dream to reconnect her with her childhood, a time of hope before pressure was exerted on her daily life, a parent may find herself feeling overwhelmed with despair. Re-connection with the Great Mother archetype blesses us with receptivity to the renewable energy of the earth. It is a new beginning from which life and play and simplicity may re-enter the dreamer's life. Attitudes about how to live life may change and responsibilities may diminish. At this point there may come dreams of death. This death is welcome and is purely metaphorical; it implies the death of an old way of being in return for a child-like rebirth.

8

Endless Energy

Depression is a heavy cloak. It is energy misused, unused, misdirected and stagnant. It is an attitude wherein the realm of the Mother is underestimated or ignored. Awareness and gratitude are essential for the release of energy. For that which we are not grateful, no more will be given. It is Divine Mother's law.

Energy is a gift of the Great Mother. It is found in many forms right here on earth. It is fire and it is electricity. It is nuclear and explosive. It is carried on the wind, in the sea, beneath the earth and through the breath. In human form it is referred to as libido.

Libido is a topic most often commandeered by sex therapists. To some extent this is natural. It is said by ancient yogis that life is a matter of birth, sex and death. That's it. Everything, apparently, can be narrowed down to these three areas of experience. Maybe Freud was not so far off the mark. Libido, however, is energy. The study of energy is divided into two camps. First, "the mechanistic view is purely causal; it conceives an event as the effect of a cause, in the sense that unchanging substances change their relations to one another, according to fixed laws." Second, "the energetic point of view . . . is in essence final; the event is tracked back from effect to cause on the assumption that some kind of energy underlies the changes."[1] Thus, according to these two views, energy is caused by the occurrence of an outside event or, conversely, the event is manufactured within us.

A third view is yogic and comes from the kundalini system. This view is allied more closely with the laws of quantum physics, a view that also resonated with Jung. This view maintains that energy is always a neutral phenomenon. Only when it is out of balance does it cause a stir. When it pertains to our bodies and our libidos, it is rarely of any concern unless it is out of balance, that is, unless our energy is too low or too high. Listless, sad, even depressive behavior is energy out of control. The neutral state is that of reflection, meditation and peace. Excess libido manifests in those symptoms of constant motion, hyper-vigilance and disturbed wellbeing.

Obviously, energy exists within matter. As bodies we are aware of the balance or imbalance of our energy in direct relation to our body awareness. In turn, body awareness extends to earth awareness and once again we find ourselves in the realm of the Great Mother. Consequently, our libido or our access to energy is ours to regulate. How we breathe, move, eat and look at this earth is up to us. When I hear someone in my practice say, "I can't change my behavior," for instance, I must ask the logical question. "Then who can, or who will, if not you?" We are in charge of that energy balance unless there is a grave physiological impairment to that energy.

Attitude comes under the category of libido balance. Focus and direction of energy can be a function of attitude. Without direction energy will be wasted, that is, spun in a circle and returned to the earth. Stasis, that idyllic state in mother's belly, is an infant state. Evolution beyond birth in the form of growth on many levels is hard work. Our personality type, our basic temperament and the environment all make use of different portions of our energy. This is inevitable and part of the price we pay to rent our space on earth. However, energy can be transformed and directed. Rather than stay with habitual patterns of the unconscious we can transform the energy we are allotted at conception into a positive direction. This is a fundamental tenet of Buddhist philosophy.

Symbols used as reminders and myths told as lessons help us to channel our attitudes. We can use them to our benefit rather than for our destruction. Today we recognize the use of meditation practice in the treatment of depression. Psychotherapy and meditation have been found to be as effective as medication. It is an accepted fact that medications mask the symptoms of depression. When a severely depressed person has no motivation or energy, medication can act as a jump starter to lift symptoms of severe depression. However, it is necessary for the person to delve into the actual reason for the low energy or the imbalance. When the cloud of depression has lifted the real work on the neglected psyche must begin.

In past centuries libido, neurosis and sexual malfunction were all grouped in the same category and what was called for was simple self-control. When psychoanalysis first explored the realm of the unconscious dreams were uncovered. Initially, Freud's followers were accused of unethical motives and the promotion of licentious behavior because Freud concentrated on libido in the realm of sexuality. Later, C. G. Jung expanded the horizons of psychoanalysis by studying the libido in regard to energy, potential and balance. Jung's study of kundalini yoga and its detailed evaluation of energy in its many manifestations increased Western knowledge of the libido. Then the examination of libido was no longer confined to the field of sexuality. Energy became the focus of physics, psychology, engineering and mathematics. Though it was still invisible its manifestations could be seen more clearly. It was realized that energy could be moved; it could be worked with and grasped by the conscious mind.

In respect to the libido's mind connection, it may be noted that a series of minor psychic shocks, attained over a lifetime, adds up to a kind of numbness that seeps from mind to body. These small traumas add up. Of course, the storage depot is the body, the unconscious and the domain of the mother. Where else can we store all the information we perceive as shocks?

We know today from the field of neuroscience that the brain is like an old movie on a double reel. One reel stores all the incoming incidents that happen to us. The other reel interprets each incident in a way that gives meaning to the event. It helps to categorize and make sense of the sensory input. The first reel rolls over and deposits this information to the rational side of the brain, which then takes these incidents and makes sense of them, organizes them and translates this information in an interpretive way on a big screen. Here we can connect to past experiences and learn by adding to our knowledge. If the incidents coming in are in any way traumatic, as for example, in the case of veterans back from the war, people exposed to death and violent behavior, accidents of a life threatening nature or insults to personal integrity or abilities, there will be a disconnect in the reels. What happens is that the information storage area continues to store the information while the body helps out with the overload. What does not happen is information transmission to the second reel. A bridge is needed for that transformation. In the brain the bridge is known as the *corpus collosum.* It is brain matter that connects one side of the brain to the other side. Once these sides are reconnected energy can be channeled more clearly.

In the kundalini system there are designated chakras or representative energy centers in the body, seven in all. These begin in the area of the perineum and go to the crown of the head along the spinal axis. Symbolically these centers denote energetic values that encompass everything from sexuality and fear to self-realization. Thus, the first and most basic chakra is the one that deals with fear. It is located at the bottom of the unknown from whence fear arises. This chakra contains the unconscious. Sex, creation, survival and our basic instincts are manifest at this energetic level.

In the actual body the first chakra is symbolized to reside at the base of the sex organs near the end location of the digestive system. The kundalini chakra chart that Carl Jung kept hung in his office is explained by Jungian analytical psychologists as esoteric and symbolic. One forgets that kundalini wisdom includes as one of its major paths the study of hatha yoga. This is the form of yoga preferred in the West. Hatha yoga is characterized by gymnastic poses used to keep the body flexible. The postures or asanas, as they are called, developed over thousands of years and once were performed with purpose and for reasons that were not cosmetic or gymnastic. Many asanas have the names of animals or of other archetypal forms such as the mountain or triangle. These asanas, in turn, were meant to unlock stored or potential energies from various locations in the body. In yoga classes it is not unusual to have to take aside someone who has touched on and released one of these key spots and begun to cry. Tears released by the body are a welcome letting go of trapped emotions and energy. They can free the system to work more efficiently. In the language of monastics, whose work on inner and spiritual life is a daily task, the locked energy and the process of releasing this inner strength is referred to as the *via negativa*. The Divine is known only through energy, by what cannot be said. It is beyond the comprehension of the mind. It is a mystical phenomenon found in all world religions. Its presence confirms the limitations of ordinary perception.

We acquire our normal everyday attitudes, which release or trap energy, honestly. Because the body does not have many means by which to speak to us it is pretty much ignored or maltreated. In no other culture has the body been so abused or pushed around as in ours. Our demands on our bodies are nearly superhuman. Take note of the next Olympic games, for instance, or watch your neighbor at the gym. Imagine the internal organs of some of the customers in fast food lines or the steroid effect on athletes. In the book that is a compendium of our life, it is the body that remembers and recognizes what our minds cannot comprehend. Thus, we demonstrate compassion for ourselves when we treat our bodies with gentle reverence.

In hatha yoga one of the essential asanas for balanced body health is the bridge pose. In this position the area of the body that is raised up and exposed is the abdomen, the solar plexus. The energy of this chakra is sight. You have certainly heard the expression, "Her eyes are bigger than her stomach." Work concentrated on this area brings up many important issues such as what we hunger for, what we see that we want, what fulfills us and so forth. It is also connected to the aspect of the brain that relates to vision. What would I like to see more clearly in my life? What image arises with an emotional undertone? Maybe it is a recurring image or one that appears in my dream. Certain asanas cause pressure on body organs located in the areas of this particular chakra. This pose, in turn, may release the emotion attached to an image. What happens is that eye movement, which is central to current treatment for trauma, activates images attached to emotions stored on one side of the brain. Often a certain area of the body is also involved. In bridge pose the abdomen, which is a repository for many of our emotions, is lifted up. In this vulnerable position it is exposed to our fears. In this position we often hear ourselves say, "I don't like this, never did and refuse to hold on to this any longer." In this position it is nearly impossible to hide or to protect the abdomen. But it is the perfect position to transfer that emotional image to the other side of the brain, to find a new perspective on the traumatic issue and to find the courage to let it go. Once the two sides of an issue are exposed we can find a solution and deal with the problem. In hatha yoga this method deals slowly with one stored memory after another and smoothes us out into a more balanced and conscious human being.

Other asanas may touch off this abdominal wall but each asana comes at the abdomen from a different direction. The cobra pose, for one, presses down on the abdomen and lower chakras. We know that the snake crawls on its belly. It is voracious in its appetite, perhaps due to its lidless eyes that are always prone to temptation. Because its desire may arise from what it wishes to see, it must look inside. Temptation and envy come from within. There is no one else and nothing to blame when we have no self-control. It becomes a matter of insight, tuning our receptivity finely, to know without seeing or hearing, what we really want. The snake is also a symbol of wisdom. It stays close to the earth and feels the pulse of the earth's vibrations. It cannot be tricked by outer appearance or be deceived by anything it wishes to hear or see. It is very close to the mother and is the sacred symbol of kundalini yoga. It symbolizes the spine and the listening that comes directly through the body in the form of light. Furthermore, the snake sheds its skin and "this ability to shed its skin symbolizes renewal and resurrection."[2] It is "the great creative force."[3] The "celestial serpent symbolizes the rainbow and can form a bridge from this world to the next"[4]. The worlds belong to earth mother, sky father and both the right and the left side of understanding.

Aesculepius, the god of healing through dreams, carried the snake with him. The serpent coils upward and into the heavens. Its goal and purpose is to strive upward from the gut level. Spiraled from the earth while on its belly, the snake's flexible body seeks within its own inner body the wisdom to attain the heights.

During my many years of visits to Yasodhara Ashram while Swami Radha was alive, I often complained to her that it seemed to be my lot in life to exist always at the level of the first chakra. I felt mired in mundane survival fears. I struggled to find the time to write. My body was virtually numb. Hatha yoga was scary and the corpse pose literally would cause me to choke and roll over. It was not death that scared me so much, I told her, but the pain of living fully. With a history of emotional deprivation, how was I to deal with feelings? No, it was too much. "Stay where you are," she advised. "Continue to seek awareness and have patience. It will pay off eventually."

Then I had a dream. It was a lucid dream so clear and colorful that I can step into it at this very moment of writing. In the dream I am wandering in a great desert on the African continent. There is nothing around me for miles and miles. Suddenly I see an oasis and I walk toward it, parched and hoping it is not a mirage. As I get closer it looks to be full of life. A market is set up and people have appeared as if from nowhere. They are dressed colorfully and walk around noisily, enjoying life. I go from person to person, asking if anyone knows where I may find the secret recipe for making indigo blue dye. I know I have already traveled afar to places like India and other parts of Africa but no one has known the secret. An old woman in a burka comes toward me. Most of her face is covered but her eyes are mesmerizing. I beg her to tell me the secret because I know she knows the answer. Finally, she gets close and from beneath her cape her hand reaches out. She turns my palm up and smears something from her palm to mine. I look down and my palm is covered with indigo blue dye. "Wait," I call out, as she begins to fade away and disappear, "can't you tell me where you got this?" "Just stay right where you are," she whispers, "and someday you will be covered from head to toe with indigo blue." Then she is gone and no matter how I try to get her back she has simply vanished.

The willingness to live life fully begins with the taking of small steps to build confidence. The attitude needed to proceed in this patient manner is a function of slowly releasing energy from the solar plexus, gaining insight into our personal and daily situation and acknowledging how it fits into the greater vision of our earth community. In her seemingly contrary wisdom, Mother Nature's inertia and overwhelming darkness are overcome by her gifts. She sends symbols of her own nature to help us to deal with her presence. Libido, in its weakened state, gazes at the difficulties of life on earth. Building character is a never-ending process. It is a rising up with great effort and courage to face each day and its challenges, to change those negative moments into light and healing vision, to lift up like the serpent that avoids temptation and that listens from within to the sound of creation.

One symptom of misplaced libido is overeating. Hunger for mother becomes an anxious intake of food that cannot be controlled. The belly begins to grow and the entire digestive tract becomes involved. The chakra energy at the level of the gut becomes obstructed. In the practice of kundalini yoga chakras that are obstructed are directed to release sacred energy. The kundalini serpent is known as the serpent of fire. Part of the act of uncovering energy is to burn the excess body fat in a sacrificial act. This act releases energy. The act of love, for instance, redirects libido. This action can be confused with sex. Mating causes heat, therefore sex and fire are misunderstood and misused. Within the act of love is pure love itself. Sex is only one aspect of love, certainly of the limited adolescent definition of love. The true hunger is for mother's love. When we are loved we feel warm all over.

The libidinal fire that is repressed and hidden in the belly can do all sorts of damage because it does not simply go away or stay locked up. That is only our unconscious fantasy wish. In reality it begins to destroy its host. Imagine the poison of the serpent! Libido or energy needs an outlet; it needs to be re-channeled. Unfortunately, this sad energy is channeled most often into anger or anxiety. The more the origins of the subdued libido or depression are denied or kept in the dark, the worse the symptoms become. It is at this point that some people seek professional assistance. Unfortunately and too often, one finds one's self in the hands of the wrong person and the search for the source is obscured with medication or thwarted with superficial solutions or platitudes. It is never an easy fix so one must beware of those who claim it is simple. It is necessary to persevere.

Essentially, energy needs an outlet. It needs to move and to flow. Inertia is its negative aspect or its antithesis. Energy in the form of fire burns. As water, it flows. As air, it blows around. Even as earth, it often shakes and cracks, explodes or slides. Its movement is slow but its movement is growth. How then do we get trapped energy to move? The answer is in the nature of the archetype. It has the power to bridge the world of conscious awareness and the unconscious body. The archetype is a numinous or holy energy that connects both to that which we already have and to that which we know collectively.

Fire, for instance, as an archetype, is imbued with an awesome energy. Fire is often referred to as part of the passions, as sexuality, or as a spiritual event like the burning bush. In the world of kundalini and the serpent, the serpent is the harbinger of fire. That fire in the belly is the holy fire that releases trapped energy. It is ignited as speech and poetry, prayers and writings. It is the outlet of mother energy and creation, self-expression, the voice of fire and words inflamed by the spirit. "The voice of the Lord scattereth flames of fire (Jeremiah 23:29). "Is not my word like a fire?" (Revelations: 115). Sound harkens from the breath. The spoken and the written word harken from the belly of the soul. The power of the word transforms fire from mere flames of destruction to constructive and inspiring action. Psychic energy as libido looks like vitality. Vitality is the opposite of inertia and belongs to the world of Divine Mother. It is she who demands praise and worship, she who sustains us and demands in return recognition of the nourishment she has given us. We cannot use earth's food that is hers or kill that which she has created.

Therefore, the word, ascribed to Shakti in the kundalini system, is the great liberator of the psyche. The word is the fire that connects us to the dark and inner solar plexus. Fire is a messenger of the mother archetype, the great bridge between body and soul. What is more, "soma (or body) and fire are identical in Vedic literature. The ancient Hindus saw fire both as the symbol of Agni (fire) and as an emanation of the inner libido-fire."[5]

To sacrifice the libido-fire in the body is the first step in redemption. "It is the custom in the Catholic Church to light a new fire at Easter."[6] To use this fire correctly in the performance of sacrifice is a necessity.

Speech, for the sake of hearing one's self talk, is useless. It must be directed in efforts that awaken the heart and the passions. It must be drawn from the breath and inspired through the soul or the body.

Not to use these efforts in an enlightened way is tragic. Without correct attitude or intention, the libido is blocked once again or even for the first time and introversions such as an inability to live in the world, perverted fantasies, passivity, procrastination, sloth and total inertia, even catatonia and pseudo-schizophrenia can occur. Reality escapes these victims of their own misdirected energy, and the chance for an heroic existence becomes mired in demonic possession. Such human dramas are enacted every day by thousands of people who have ignored their instincts.

We must never assume that demonic forces are not lurking in the wings of our personal and private life dramas, waiting to step in and cause havoc. We must take into our own lives the decision to make of our energy something beautiful or useful or of practical value to others and to ourselves. Energy that is accessed is meant to be shared, not stored beneath a basket or locked away uncultivated.

The libido and its association with fire is combined in ancient knowledge that has come to us through collective sighs and whispers, through writings and religious texts and through the bridge that is created by dreams. Fire was once worshipped as a golden-winged bird.

The Chinese call it qi; Indians call it prana. The awakening of this subtle life energy is a mysterious process that begins at the base of the spine at the place where we sit on mother earth. Then, it travels upward. It may stop and be caught in the belly that has been blocked and overloaded, or it may continue its upward travels until it reaches the brain. How much of this energetic activity is manifest as the product of our intentions? It cannot be measured and therefore it is unreliable scientifically. Kundalini, as the fire and as the serpent's power, is best approached with caution. An ancient sage once wrote these poetic stanzas in devotion to Shakti the goddess of kundalini yoga:

O Mother: He who contemplates Thee, even for an instant . . .
O Mother: Those who meditate on Thee as the purifier . . .

O Mother: Some call Thee as Supreme Knowledge . . .
O Thou Mother of all the worlds, why speak further (about
Thy attributes)? Our only prayer is (that) Thou may manifest
thyself to us in thy supreme dark-blue aspect, like a host of
blue-water lilies with curly, moist, glistening, tawny hair and
with protruding breasts hanging down on Thy Beautiful
waist.[7]

Represented by the white-coiled serpent, kundalini yoga is experienced as jolts of lightening that travel up the spine from its base. This energy then pervades the body. It is claimed by the yogi sages that one is not spiritually awakened until this energy has been aroused in the body. The priesthood of formal religions has been aware of evidence of this mystical energy for over four thousand years. Joseph Campbell has made note of the "Book of Kells made alive with symbolic serpents . . . but also, on the side of an immense stone cross of the same pre-gothic Christian period—the 'Cross of [the abbot] Muiredach' . . . known as Dextra Dei, the 'Right Hand of God,' in which two interlacing serpents appear, one heading downward, the other upward."[8] Among the Maya and the Aztec, depiction of serpent energy resembled the kundalini serpent coiled around the spine. The Navajo sand painting from the blessing chant depicts the same spiritual knowledge also shown in Tibetan sand paintings. The point is that this awakening is taught and monitored to those who practice kundalini through spiritual exercises. They can be learned. The priesthood does not have exclusive claim to them. Caution, hard work and sincerity are required in order to use this power effectively. Indiscriminate experimentation with this knowledge was tried during the sixties in the hippie culture but its use was tampered with frequently, for right or wrong reasons, and caused reactions that resembled schizophrenia. Today the DSM criteria for categories of mental illness acknowledge a "spiritually induced psychosis".[9] Unfortunately, only a select few practitioners are able to detect this state of mind based on the client's history. In undertaking spiritual exercises, motivation or intention must be pure. To use the exercises for the entertainment of psychedelic lights, bells and whistles is inappropriate and may simply cause a whole new set of problems. These additional problems may be of critical concern in the form of lowered libido or severe depression:

It is said that what we experience in our lives depends to a certain degree upon the chakra to which we are attuned, for each chakra is energized by certain emotional, mental, psychic, and spiritual attributes. Those who are in touch with the lower chakras will be more inclined to find and seek fulfillment through gratification of the physical senses, and those who have opened the gateways to the higher chakras will aspire toward intellectual and spiritual attainments.[10]

Those who practice kundalini safely and sincerely are rewarded with a connection to the source of all creation, the soul-mother of kindness and love. Once this connection has been made, libido problems dissolve; the world is once and for all filled with color and life.

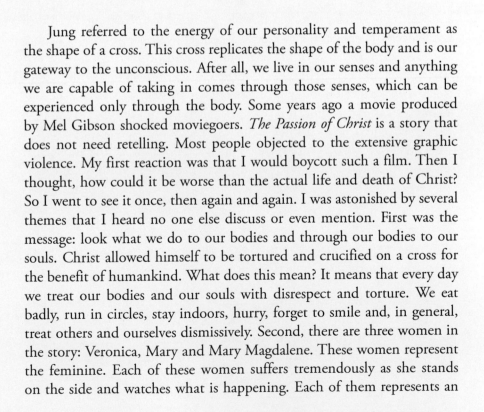

Jung referred to the energy of our personality and temperament as the shape of a cross. This cross replicates the shape of the body and is our gateway to the unconscious. After all, we live in our senses and anything we are capable of taking in comes through those senses, which can be experienced only through the body. Some years ago a movie produced by Mel Gibson shocked moviegoers. *The Passion of Christ* is a story that does not need retelling. Most people objected to the extensive graphic violence. My first reaction was that I would boycott such a film. Then I thought, how could it be worse than the actual life and death of Christ? So I went to see it once, then again and again. I was astonished by several themes that I heard no one else discuss or even mention. First was the message: look what we do to our bodies and through our bodies to our souls. Christ allowed himself to be tortured and crucified on a cross for the benefit of humankind. What does this mean? It means that every day we treat our bodies and our souls with disrespect and torture. We eat badly, run in circles, stay indoors, hurry, forget to smile and, in general, treat others and ourselves dismissively. Second, there are three women in the story: Veronica, Mary and Mary Magdalene. These women represent the feminine. Each of these women suffers tremendously as she stands on the side and watches what is happening. Each of them represents an aspect of Divine Mother and of the soul's torment. Their daily suffering, I thought, was the true reason for Christ's sacrifice; for our greatest sin is our failure to uphold matter that is the essence of creation. Even a symbol like Christ, whose name means light, has not generated enough in the way of this specific awareness. Must there be darkness in order to see the light? Where are we, each and every one of us in this light spectrum?

Is it any wonder that depression or lowered libido accounts for more disability than heart disease? Is it a surprise that death by suicide is the first cause of injury-based death for people aged twenty-five to sixty-four?[11] I often recall the Peace Corps, for which I worked in Africa. *Corps de la paix*: in French these words continue to reverberate in my mind: body of peace, body of peace. Initially, the Peace Corps was primarily a language and cultural exchange program with minimal emphasis on technical excellence. College students taught English in exchange for friendship and greater understanding of other cultures and people. It was an effort at good will and caring on behalf of the Great Mother, and in the 1960s and 1970s it educated many young people in greater open mindedness. It was worth an entire education to learn greater appreciation for what we already have and how to share it. It was also about learning how much others truly already have. I learned that we do not have all the answers. A sense of peace and harmony enters my being when I realize I do not have answers.

To learn about the cross that Jung described in relation to personality and that Christ carried as a prelude to his bodily death has been of far greater benefit for me than almost any other act of learning that I can recall. It was easy for me to discover what personality type I could be described as. I am an overtly feeling type personality for better or worse. Following that acceptance, my second most developed function is intuition. But this, I was soon to learn, did not help me to understand the sensate function which, for me, is my shadowy unconscious. Nor did it help me to understand the thinking function that falls into the inferior axis of my personality cross.

When Jung described personality types and used the cross as a descriptor of the actions of the four personality functions, he used the third arm of the cross to depict one's shadow function: a third function in each person that would normally remain in an obscure or even annoyingly negative state of awareness for a lifetime. It would represent all those attributes that were so close to a state of awareness that one could almost but never quite grasp.

My third function is sensate and dwells in a shadowy, uncomfortable state. To a person with a highly developed sensate function, machines, directions, space and the ground are all understandable, knowledge gained through the five main senses. The body is a wondrous machine. The great dancers of the world are often sensate types. They know where they are in space.

As for my coordination, it is not my strong suit. Computers are anathema and frighten me. If I cannot see it, it is sure to disappear. Deprivation is a shadowy state, a void wherein negativity and self-pity may dwell easily. The opposite of deprivation is gratitude, plenitude and devotion. Add deprivation to the lack of sensate awareness, and I dwell in a land of wavering reality. Groups of people remain a sea of faces. One-to-one is a better connection for me. Letters rather than emails enhance my finer feelings. Telephone calls rather than text messages ground my communications. And hatha yoga rather than a treadmill deepens my awareness of my own body. I need to be up close and personal.

Devotion must appeal directly to my senses. Consequently, mantra, aloud and sung, works better than the lost void of silent meditation to deepen my consciousness in the inner journey leading to a higher self. Colorful tankas, wrinkly malas, sandalwood incense, lighted candles in reflective prism-like holders absorb and hold my attention better if they are right in my face. I need to be surrounded with reminders. Statues and photos, music and flowers fill each room in my home. These objects ground me. They help me add on to the past years of scarcity and muted input. They help me to catch up to my own potential understanding of the world. Rather than feeling sorry for myself, I am motivated by them to explore and to expand my consciousness. Roses, in particular, help me to unlock my fears and to move ahead into the unknown. I keep them on my desk at all times as a constant reminder of the heart of any issue. They transcend the obvious senses.

The attitude acquired through devotions like meditation, mantra, prayer or contemplation begins with the physical action itself. Just do it. Look at the tanka you place in the hallway or at the little statue near the bathroom sink. Smell the rose you place beside the bed or the plate of food on the table. Get on your knees and bend over in the dear position of the small child. Touch your forehead to the floor, the earth, the grass, the sand, the concrete or the tree root. Begin right now. The buck stops here. If you have food in your mouth savor it, taste it, appreciate what you have and give a thought to someone who is starving. Say a heartfelt prayer for them.

The discerning cognitive psychologist, Aaron Beck, asked his clients to question concepts they had held dear all their lives. Yoga inquiry that is a component of kundalini yoga has asked this same question for thousands of years. Ask if the scowling person across the room is angry or sad or defensive or simply lonely. Don't jump at the first concept that enters your mind. Are you unloved or do people feel you are holding off their overtures? Do you like yourself? Today, did you do something you like? Do you also feel sorry for yourself? If so, why? What can you do to make the day happier, more peaceful or satisfying? What one little thing can you do? Can you write a little poem the way Emily Dickenson did? Can you knit a blanket for a newborn child who might have to be wrapped in newspaper without your little blanket? That is what my mother-in-law did, when she lived in Mexico and could not speak Spanish. Can you buy someone a coffee, then sit and have coffee with them?

Recently a young client came to me, crying. She was trying to save her little nephew whom she looked after, her mother who was a drug addict, and her boyfriend who had been traumatized. She was anxious and worried about getting through her last year of university. She was doing things for everyone else and nothing for herself. This is not what I mean by asking, 'What can I do?' The question is meant to inquire into motivation and the correct release of stored and misused energy. Of course, I took on the role of inquisitor. What had she done for herself that day? Fortunately, she had come to see me. It was a start. Underneath all this giving away of energy and potential, she knew what I would advise and what I would ask. She just needed confirmation. Others have buried their own needs much deeper, unfortunately.

Energy must be used wisely. It is a gift of the Great Mother. The question, "Where is mother?" is answered through an acceptance of what we have been given. Our own special and unique gift is our life, and this may be our one and only chance to evolve and to reach awareness. How will we use this life energy? We have all been mothers before. Whether we remember how to mother others or we have forgotten, we must know how to mother ourselves. We have a responsibility to care for and to nurture the gift of being here in the presence of earth's energy, for here in its vital center is mother.

9

Mother of the Dawn
Madonna &Transformation

To transform is to go beyond an old form or way of being into a new one. From trapped to free, from depressed to energized, from shapeless to sculpted. As any sculptress can tell you, the form was already in the stone, awaiting discovery and attention. We find our forms in unique ways, the way stone child did. For me, mother metamorphosed into Divine Mother from the form of the Black Madonna who is mother of us all.

Often the catalyst for transformation begins with the archetypal image. As a collectively understandable symbol, the archetype inherits a numinous glow, a holy and awesome aura that touches the heart and soul. It inspires reverence and devotion.

In my own life this catalyst appeared as Divine Mother. I will spend the greater part of this chapter describing some of these encounters and how they came about. I have already mentioned my home life and the church I attended as a child: St. Mary's, Our Lady of Czestochowa. Her icon was prominent as I entered the church. There, she faced me near the holy water as I blessed myself. I mentioned my innocent conversations with Mary, who was modeled after the Pieta, as well as with the elevated and light-shining lady on the pedestal that we crowned every May to commemorate the month of Mary. These images were a part of my childhood and obviously had had years to incubate in silent darkness.

Many years later, on the day my letter of acceptance arrived from the C. G. Jung Institute in Kusnacht, Switzerland, there arrived a brief note from a woman I had once met at Yasodhara Ashram. She was devoted to Mary. The note said that Mary had asked her to give me a particular photo that had been taken outside the church of Medjugori near Poland. The photo is extraordinary. There, in the photo, is the image of a Madonna of light, and this Madonna is standing on a beautiful rainbow of white light. I have kept this photo on my desk all these years because the light from the photo is palpable and strong. It is undeniably holy. The moment I opened the envelope and gazed at the image was the moment my real journey began.

Shortly after, I arrived in Kusnacht, a week before classes started. My intention was to settle in and find my way around the city. As I stood on the train platform in town a few days after my arrival, I met a friendly American woman. Bonnie Greenwell was part of the kundalini network in the United States at that time, a psychologist who had decided to visit the Jung Institute to attend public lectures. Together, we decided to explore the world of China Galland who had recently written *Longing for Darkness*. In her poignant odyssey Galland had traveled to Einsiedeln in Switzerland where she discovered the Black Madonna. This Madonna, in turn, had strengthened Bonnie's connection to the goddess Tara. Strangely enough, Bonnie and I had both read the book but the Einsiedeln connection had not stayed in my mind. That day I was introduced to Our Lady of the Hermits, the oldest of the Black Madonnas in Europe. Her statue at Einsiedeln dates back to the ninth century. It was the day I fell in love. At afternoon vespers held in the main church every monk in the monastery filed in procession to the entrance of the basilica. There they lined up in front of the Black Madonna and sang the *Salve Regina*.

I listen as the monks sing in rising voices of reverence. I feel joy and sorrow. It never fails to set me in a valley of tears then raise me up in hope:

> Hail, Holy Queen, mother of mercy, our life, our sweetness
> and our hope. To thee do we cry, poor banished children of
> Eve. To thee do we send up our sighs, mourning and weeping
> in this valley of tears. Turn then, most precious mother, your
> eyes of mercy toward us. And after this, our exile, show us

the blessed fruit of thy womb, Jesus. O clement, O loving,
O sweet Virgin Mary.

The a cappella voices raised in song were magnificent. Every afternoon these devout Benedictine monks perform this same ritual to Divine Mother. It is their comfort, their strength and their sustenance.

The dark feminine is met with light as we gaze at each other. She is a continuum of experience of light and dark energy. This interior activity is not without its dangers but the rewards in terms of release of the libido energy and the activity that can ensue are tremendous. In the kundalini system this activity is the equivalent of Shakti's union with Siva. Their union gives birth to the appearance of spring and new life. It is not only the emergence of consciousness but is directed at new growth and at a collaborative release from inertia. These transformations have been the delight of civilization, for "these manifestations of the Archetypal Feminine in all times and all cultures, that is, among all human beings of the prehistoric and historical worlds, appear also in the living reality of the modern woman, in her dreams and visions, compulsions and fantasies, projections and relationships, fixations and transformations."[1] Basically this means that, when the feminine kundalini energy of the body meets with the more subtle masculine energy, a mysterious alchemy takes place. In the recognition of contributions to the evolution of humankind, there is cooperation, and the use of energy becomes clearly focused. It is like the connection of the transmission of a car that allows the car to be put in motion:

> With the emergence of something soul-like—the anima—from the archetypal feminine, the unconscious, not only does a change occur in the relations of ego to unconscious and of man to woman, but the action of the unconscious within the psyche also assumes new and creative forms. While the elementary character of the feminine tends to dissolve the ego and consciousness in the unconscious,

160

the transformative character of the anima fascinates but does not obliterate it; it sets the personality in motion, produces change and ultimately transformation."[2]

For the next three years that I was a student at the Jung Institute, I was also a devotee of the Black Madonna. Oftentimes on my way to lectures, I would find myself instead on a train to Einsiedeln. My analyst Dr. Ian Baker often asked me if I had come to Zurich to study Jung's work or to become acquainted with the Madonna. There were times when I arrived in Einsiedeln in the afternoon just before vespers but it did not feel like enough time to savor the holiness there. So I would find a hotel and stay a day or two just to be in her presence. I was so grateful to have found her.

One day I saw a busload of people from India getting out of their bus in front of the church, and I stopped to ask them how they had heard of this place. They replied that they had come to visit the great Kali in her Madonna manifestation. She had told them of her existence. They were not Catholics but had made this pilgrimage from half way around the world.

"Do you pray?" Ian once asked me. "What do you do there?" "I just sit and wait," I told him. "I wait in silence." This, I was later to discover, is the essence of prayer. It is also meditation. In the Madonna's presence, nothing else is required.

In my second semester at the Institute I attended a free concert at a lovely old Lutheran church near Paradaplatz. With my old friend Siri Ness I sat in rapture, listening to a Poulenc concerto. The music was glorious but what happened during the concert was unforgettable. Suddenly the figure of Mary appeared before me, larger than life, covered in newspaper print with headlines of tragedies covering her gown. She moved toward me, holding out an infant whose clothes were dripping with blood. "Look,"

she lamented, "Look what we do to the children." I came out of my trance some time later, a bit dazed, and listened to the musical finale before we stood and left the church. Siri noted that at one point I had seemed far away and transported, but I was not ready to share my vision. Instead, we went to the Savoy piano bar, had a martini and dined on free peanuts and olives. Such is the student's life. I kept this incident in my own heart for quite a while, selfishly perhaps, but intent on absorbing in silence the message and the awe. This is no easy task for an extrovert.

What I discovered in my silent incubation of this dark image was a *temenos* of great safety and solitude. I went through my days and even the lectures at the Institute in transports of ecstasy. Many loose strings and random events that had occurred in my life began to gather; my ego, which had been ignored by my family during my childhood and my early years, took on a strength that I somehow recognized in the center of this sacred and protected space. Here, I had the time and the opportunity to gather myself and, strangely, I did not even share this event with my beloved analyst.

I went home that year for the winter break, back to my family and friends, who had missed me. But I was home only a short while when the phone rang. A group of women was putting together a show at the university called *Images of the Goddess*. It was to be a collaborative art experience, and they invited me to take part. They needed someone who would present Mary as a goddess! Someone I did not know had given them my name. This was a bit unusual, so I was sure there was some mistake. However, they entreated me to come to their planning session, to meet them and discuss the project before flatly refusing to participate. Reluctantly, I went to their meeting and, before it ended, heard myself say that I would represent the Black Madonna with a sculpture. Where I would find time in the months before the show, I had no idea. My daughter then stepped in to sustain me with her creative spirit. I went back to Zurich for the new semester and the next summer, with her help, I created a six foot six inch, *papier mache* sculpture. I commissioned a sixteen-note mantra to play in the background of the display, and this composition was also used as the theme music of the program. It suited the occasion perfectly. The paper for the sculpting was, of course, newspaper—seven full layers of it. I could not help but remember my vision of Mary with the terrible newspaper headlines. I painted over the paper but the child she held out was a sacrifice and an offering, its clothes dripping with red paint. That show went on to win the North American Crystal Award for teachers that year. The mantra was used in the documentary that was made of the installation and show at the University of Calgary. We sold out for all three days of the exhibit and I went home oddly comforted.

I will also share some unusual incidents that happened while this process was under way. The week before the installation of the show, no one was willing to transport the sculpture from my home to the university. I was told that because they considered the sculpture a valuable work of art, no moving company would risk the liability. At that time the sculpture was valued at thousands of dollars. Finally, a mover responded to my desperate plea and agreed to make a house call to examine the work. What happened was not so strange when I consider what had happened to me during the Poulenc concert. The fellow walked into my home and ignored me the moment he spotted the Madonna in my living room. He walked in, circled her and mumbled, "What is this? What is this?"

I sat on a nearby sofa and watched as he was transported someplace else. Then he sat beside me on the sofa and began to cry. No, he was not a Catholic. No, he had never heard of a Black Madonna. His tears were for his earlier life when he had abused a first wife and children. Now he was remarried and this young and beautiful wife was about to have his child. What kind of husband and father would he be in the years to come? He cried in remorse for the past and in fear of the future. "What is this?" he asked again. "You already know in your heart," I told him. "She is forgiveness. How you forgive yourself this very moment in front of her, and the healing that comes from this experience will determine the future and the happiness of you, your wife and child." He continued to weep and I found some tissue. Then he announced that he wanted to transport the sculpture for free and would be there the next day to pick it up.

Well, he arrived with his truck, which was not high enough to accommodate the statue, and with an assistant, who was to stand in the back of the vehicle to secure the Madonna with blue satin ribbons. We drove slowly across town in tandem, with a slow procession gathering as dozens of cars slowed to follow in a line behind us. Something about the whole experience still feels like a small miracle.

During the installation of the show another incident occurred. Someone was watching me set up and I began to feel uncomfortable. That person was an old Cree woman, an elder who had come from Saskatchewan at the request of a First Nations woman in our group. An aboriginal exhibit was part of the project, in the form of a talking circle for women. It was the circle leader who watched me. I finally introduced myself to Victoria and her son, who was obviously training to be a healer. On opening night Victoria was asked to say a prayer before we opened the doors to the public. Many people waited in the foyer, their excitement apparent through the glass entrance. However, Victoria was not to be hurried. As part of her prayer she wanted to tell us the story of her vision quest. First she told her story in Cree and then in English.

"I went to the top of a mountain for three days without food or water or shelter," she told us. "But at the end of the third day God had not given me a vision and I was sad. I turned to leave the mountain and at my first step, God shouted, 'Stop.' I looked around, confused because that was it, nothing more. Again, I took a step. 'Stop,' he shouted, louder than before. I fell to my knees and cried and bowed my head to the earth and then for some reason I started to dig, right there in the ground, with my hands. This is what I found." She reached into her pocket and took out an exquisitely polished black onyx stone in the shape of a Madonna. She turned in my direction, looked me in the eye and said, "So it is a very good thing you do." She then proceeded to say more prayers in Cree and the doors were opened to the exhibit. I never had another chance to see her or to talk to her, and it was not necessary to do so. Truly, she had recognized in her heart the essence of the Black Madonna. As for me, I was no longer surprised by these unexpected occurrences.

These days, when a client comes to me with issues that seem somewhat perplexing or if we have come to an impasse in therapy, I take the hand-carved Black Madonna that I purchased in Einsiedeln the last time I was there and set it on a lovely table in my practice room. Beside her I place roses. Then I sit and wait. Inevitably, that day when my client walks in, there is communication between him or her and the Madonna. I try to stay out of the way. It is something that is beyond my comprehension but I am smart enough to know it is a profound and healing interaction that takes place.

Today, because of a request from a Cree friend whom I met during that same exhibit, I have come to work with First Nations people each week at a nearby reservation. As I mentioned earlier, I work as their trauma specialist and dream catcher. Because the process of Truth and Reconciliation has begun in Canada, I see victims of residential school abuse on a regular basis. Emotional deprivation and a lifetime of numbness are the rule rather than the exception on the reserve, but I see in these people their courage and their perseverance. Occasionally, they come in to town to see me in my home.

At home I have my private analytical practice. There, my focus in therapy is readjusted. Survival issues recede as we deal with issues that have to do with meaning of life, potential and creativity. I am blessed in being able to do this work that spans the first five chakras. I continue to work on my own first chakra, knowing now that it is trust in this process that allows me to see people each day to offer hope.

Recently, after a particularly heart wrenching session with a man broken in body and very nearly in spirit, and a two-day Truth and Reconciliation meeting, I walked to my local coffee shop to read and to write some balancing poetry. Next to me sat a young woman who was on her computer with what looked like an academic document. I sat with my poetry and coffee for an hour until the little voice in my head was appeased. It kept saying, "Ask her what her thesis is about." "Well," she said, "it is about a pilgrimage to Lac St. Anne that is made by First Nations people each year. Most of the people went to residential schools and continue to worship at the shrine of St. Anne." I was invited to her thesis presentation the next day at the university where I heard about some of the history of the Oblate Fathers in the Province of Alberta and in particular the history of this pilgrimage. As this was an historical presentation, it was as unbiased as could be expected from the obvious facts and interviews.

However, I left saddened. The real story of trauma and abuse was never told to this young woman because the elders would never talk about these traumas to a nice young white woman. It is simply not done. The issues are dealt with in traditional ceremonies and maybe even in front of St. Anne, but what I learned inadvertently was that this location had once, before the arrival of the Oblate fathers, been a very sacred site, a holy *temenos*. There, in the shallow lake, had existed a black stone, perhaps a meteorite that had fallen from the sky long ago and which was worshipped for its dark, holy and mysterious connection to the Creator. Even this was then taken from the First Nations people, as the church had it removed from the lake and placed in a museum. Cries and lamentations did not stop the priests from taking this soul-stone from the devil worshippers. Instead of abandoning this site of worship, native people come to the site each summer to continue their traditional ceremonies. They are able, somehow, to discriminate between the holy and the non-holy in a knowing and instinctive way. Nobody has robbed them of their spirit or of their connection to the Mother Creator.

Though scarcely known to exist, representations of the Black Madonna are located in hundreds of sites around the world. France, alone, is home to three hundred of these sites. However, in most cases, the Black Madonna has been painted over, camouflaged as a pure, innocent and naïve Mary, white-skinned and blue-eyed. The church has ordered these paint-overs. On my visit to Chartres, near Paris, specifically to visit one of the most famous of the Black Madonnas, I deliberately took a guided tour of the cathedral. More than half way through the tour, I had not heard one word about the Madonna, so I asked the official guide where she was. I was informed that she, the guide, had never heard of such a statue at Chartres. Of course it was there. I had merely to ask an old woman, a local, who had come to pray before her. She had not been painted over, simply ignored.

Yet in the center of France, at Le Puy, the Black Madonna is not only still venerated but parishioners and monks alike attest to bells ringing and to unusual, ethereal emanations that are given off by the Madonna whenever there are bad storms in the Mediterranean Sea and sailors are in trouble. In Poland, the Black Madonna has been venerated from as far back as the fifteenth century, when invaders were driven back from the monastery fortress at Cestochowa, until modern times, when it became a sign among those who supported solidarity. In Mexico, Our Lady of Guadeloupe has given solace to hundreds of thousands of pilgrims whose lives are impoverished. She reaches beyond their imposed Catholicism to a more universal forgiveness. Instead of the mantra, "Lord I am not worthy," she imparts wholeness and the knowledge that we are all alike in the eyes of God. In Iceland, the shamans who heal the body-soul know the Black Madonna. In Mexico, just a decade ago, a new sighting appeared. She is known as Our Lady of the Hidalgo Metro.

Just after the sighting, a short article about the event appeared in the Washington Post. A friend in Washington, D.C. cut it out and sent it to me. I boarded a plane to Mexico City to see for myself. To anyone who has not been there, the Hidalgo Metro is a busy place, with nine entrances and exits to and from the underground trains. It did not escape me that the Black Madonna chose to appear beneath the surface of the earth. The story goes that there was a stabbing fatality in the early morning hours and a subway cleaner found an unknown, dead body. When police removed the body there was a lot of blood on the tiled floor, so a cleaning woman was told to mop it up. Taking her mop, bucket and soap, she began to scrub the floor but her efforts were of no avail. There remained on the floor a blood-brown stain in the shape of the Madonna. By morning, news of this phenomenon had spread among the poor and disenfranchised throughout the city. A miracle had occurred. It became necessary for the Mexico City authorities to cordon off the area to create order. Daily, thousands of pilgrims file through the Hidalgo metro station to pray and to be blessed by the Black Madonna. Her presence exists in an image on the floor.

So what is the Madonna, brown-black and sooty image of the mother of God, all about? Why does she inspire such devotion and gratitude in her followers, who love her?

One day, as I was standing at the train station in Kusnacht in a reverie of desire to be at Einsiedeln instead of in a class at the Institute, a woman approached me and asked if I spoke English. She was newly arrived in Switzerland and planned to go to the mountains to a village called Einsiedeln. We decided to travel together, and I promptly cut classes. This woman was a Catholic who belonged to a group she referred to as part of the Marian movement. I had never heard of them but that was not unusual, as I have never subscribed to church politics or trends. Charismatics and fundamentalists from any faith make me nervous. However, I asked her about their purpose and about what they believed. They adored Mary. It was as simple as that. She told me that the Marian movement has resurfaced throughout our Christian era any time there has been an imbalance in the church structure or when the patriarchy has become overwhelming in its power or influence. The Marian followers intend that Mary never be forgotten in her role as goddess and mother of God.

Such feminine awareness in the Church is certainly in keeping with Jung's reflection. In 1956 the Vatican took decisive action, declaring the assumption of Mary to heaven. The Feast of the Assumption is celebrated each year in August. The elevation in status of Christ's mother has become an evolutionary gesture in the church. Jung believed it would be the cause of much change. Living so close to Our Lady of Hermits in Switzerland, Jung was aware of the inevitable impact that such an action would create in the church structure. He was quite close to the hermit archetype himself and lived in seclusion at Bollingen during the last years of his life.

So what are the implications of Mary's assumption into heaven? Fred Gustafson, in his important work *The Black Madonna*, defines the inner journey that brings peace amidst chaos, the journey that Jung defines as leading to the higher self. The monastic or hermitic life is not a turning away from humankind but a turning inward toward the collective and the unconscious, toward the mystery and meaning of life. It is an alchemical undertaking that points to transformation and evolution, to a vision of what we can become. It is not a fantastical voyage but one grounded in reflection, prayer and sacrifice. Its hardships include a vision of evil as well as of goodness. It is a glimpse into the personal and the collective shadow. Thus, in the case of the Black Madonna, we speak of the symbolic meaning of her blackness, her darkness.

The white Madonna of church history is depicted as virtuous and pure. It is left to Mary Magdalene, the whore and unworthy one, to represent the dark side. Though the Magdalene is an aspect of Mary, the innocent, her carnal knowledge is earth-bound and sullied. Only the Magdalene represents the higher and lower nature, indisputably a part of each of us. Some say it is she who is really the Black Madonna. In his book *Blessed and Beautiful: Picturing the Saints* Robert Kiely shows us artistic depictions of Mary Magdalene as the ambiguous repository of blame, shame and repentance for our harsh treatment of Christ. He also shows in historic art renditions how we can, through the reality of various scenes from her life, learn to understand our own shortcomings and how we are forgiven. The art inspired by her life is some of the most alive and profound in history.

This Mary is associated with night and the world of dreams. She is the healer of the spirit. She has survived fire and is honed to a shiny black renewal of strength. Her onyx blackness is of the earth and so black it shines. She does not discriminate the colors of her followers and admits to being Kali as well as every goddess who has ever stood for goodness. She awakens creative forces that have been submerged in our depths. Her energy emerges from depression and oppression. She cannot be kept buried, as the native elder demonstrated in her vision quest. Her blackness is at the bottom of the alchemical cauldron in the *prima materia* where the first chakra boils. In the Gnostic gospel of Mary she is the first to whom the risen Lord appears when he leaves the tomb. Back to the first chakra, it is here that circumstances and attitudes are acquired that direct or re-direct energy up through the spinal channels and into the heart and mind. In the boiling cauldron are both the struggle to be born and the melting back into death.

I harken back to my many dreams of the black women who walk the earth, barefooted and grounded not only in the joys but also in the adversities of life. These women know first hand about birth and death. In the African desert where I worked, children were not named until age five because of the high infant mortality rate. "The archetypal womb of death destroying what has been born,"[3] vividly demonstrates the struggle for consciousness. These women use the energy of their children to continue to live and to survive. They accept death and sorrow; they see and feel the short story that is our life on earth.

I am reminded of a visit to Ethiopia that coincided with the month of Miriam. In the ancient kingdom of Axum I was awakened just before dawn. What was it? I was suddenly alert. I got up and looked out the window to the pre-dawn light that covered the hillside and the white figures that glided through the cloud shadows and between boulders. Unable to stay, looking out, I dressed quietly and left our room. Then I heard the eerie sound of the ram's horn calling us to prayer. I, too, glided down the hillside, as more and more women gathered, dressed in white, heads covered and resembling women who lived and prayed during the time of Christ. I felt transported in time as I followed them until we came to the treed yard beside the monastery where it is believed the Ark of the Covenant resides. Silently, each woman chose a tree and, when there were no more available, they lined up facing the wall of the monastery. The horn continued its haunting call and the women waited in prayer for the dawn. I stood with them until they started to move in unison to the square in front of the building, where they formed a large circle. I was pulled into the circle as the mantra to Miriam began and voices were raised to the dawn light.

Like Kali, Isis, and Demeter, the Black Madonna is considered a healer. Forgiveness is learned at her feet. Tears of righteousness are dissolved, and the stubborn holding on to ill will and surety of truth is gone in the act of forgiveness. In that is mercy toward our own darkness and our unknown selves. If I forgive you, I can forgive that part of me that judges you to be somehow less than I. In the cauldron we are one; only in the fire can I change form, or transform.

Since her assumption to heaven, Mary appears to have unleashed a momentous movement toward wholeness. In its early stages this looks like chaos and despair, yet it is Mary who adds a new dimension to the Trinity. Whether in her white or her black form, she makes a fourth or quaternity that is the symbol of wholeness, just like the cross or the mandala. When Jung made those comments in his observations soon after the Vatican announcement, he had no idea where it would lead or what this church transformation would look like. He died in 1961.

Today we see the cleansing of the church. Priests and nuns have perpetrated sexual abuse and perversions of all kinds on children, women, and the vulnerable. Intolerance and righteousness that have prevailed in the past are being aired and exposed to the light. This dissolution of what was man-made and held to be holy will be re-evaluated and held up to divine justice. Christian churches will stand renewed or will fall in their corruption, similar to corpses that return to the earth for healing and adjustment or possibly for transformation. Anything is possible once Divine Mother, the mother creator, has shifted place in our awareness. Her mandate is healing. Now that we have called on her in true sincerity she will do her work. This I believe.

As the semester went by during my studies in Zurich, my hours and days of visits to the Black Madonna accumulated. The more often I was there, the more often I wanted to be there.

Not long after my first few visits, I had an intense sensation that I needed to move, to sit elsewhere, not in front of the lovely little Black Madonna statue. As lovely as she was dressed, as adored as she was, after the chanting of the *Salve Regina* I wanted to be somewhere else. So one day I followed an old nun I had seen several times, as she disappeared behind pillars and doorways. She walked slowly through two long corridors that I felt were going downward and behind the main altar. When she came to a set of doors, she slipped inside another room and I followed.

There, beneath what seemed to be the main altar, was a tiny chapel with its own altar of great simplicity. The wicker-woven chairs and washed walls lent the impression of a stark white cave. There I sat to wait once again. Mostly women entered this room. Nuns came and left quietly. The ornate baroque basilica above us disappeared and I felt protected, as in a white cocoon. The waiting down there was easy and the distractions few. In an alcove nearby was a watery spring that seemed like more than an ordinary man-made fountain. Perhaps it was a tributary of the fountain with twelve blessing-spouts in the front of the church. Its sound soothed me and gave me strength.

One day Dr. Baker asked me if my waiting always took place in the cold and drafty basilica. I told him I had found a better place to do my waiting. I described the chapel, full of healing and of peaceful vibrations, which I had found beneath the main altar. I told him I might wait there forever. Being a devout Catholic and knowing the history of St. Meinrad, who brought the Madonna there centuries ago, Ian explained that this chapel was the original version of the chapel built by St. Meinrad. Though cathedral-like churches had been built above it and each had burned (there were three such events over time), the original was kept intact and the Madonna had always survived unscathed. For non-believers it was an explanation for her blackness. That is, it must be soot. For me it was home; I had come home at last.

In my third year at the C. G. Jung Institute, I took a walk in the hills above Einsiedeln and the monastery grounds. I did not wish to follow the trail of the Stations of the Cross but took another path that wound through the woods in pine-scented silence. On a steep hillside I stopped, unable to go on. My feeling of the numinous was so overwhelmingly beautiful I fell to my knees and bowed my forehead to the earth. These feelings were indescribable yet not enough. My heart was so full of gratitude I did not know what to do. Suddenly I found myself prostrate on the ground, my face in the leaves and pine needles, as though I could gather the earth in my arms and embrace the whole universe. Some time later, as I was picking myself up off the sacred ground, I heard footsteps in the woods. From an obscure path came two monks, carrying axes and wearing old work clothes and peaceful faces. *"Gruss Gott,"* they greeted me, as they strode past. Obviously, I was still covered in pine needles and looked somewhat disheveled but the monks pretended not to notice as they passed. "Go with God," I repeated to myself on the way down the mountainside. "Go with God. Go with God," I whispered all the way back to the chapel.

How does one describe such joy? There is nothing else like it. It is surely a gift that surpasses understanding.

How do we explain our joy or our ecstasy? In his book of descriptive reflections on the archetype of *Ecstasy*, Robert Johnson describes the scapegoat phenomenon throughout Western history. He describes the sacrificed first young goat stewed in its mother's milk, the lamb of God that symbolizes what we devalue: groups of people like Jews, women, teenagers and artists. The answer to that question, according to Johnson, is that we don't ever answer that question. We scapegoat this tremendous gift of energy. We kill the artist, the Jew and the goat, sacrifice its energy and drive it back to the underworld of the mother. This behavior is the return of a gift no matter how we try to camouflage our actions. The scapegoat is here to stay unless we recognize what it is we do wrong. We squander true ecstasy. If we think that sex or alcohol is the answer to ecstasy, we sadly undermine our capacity for joy and we settle for illusion.

Sometimes the quality of ecstasy can come to us in a dream. Most assuredly, it will come to us through our inferior personality function. As David Miller said to me, "It will come about through your thinking function." Or as Johnson relates, it will come through the soles/souls of our feet or the ground we walk on. Again and again I am reminded of the Black Madonnas in Africa who, barefoot, walk the earth in peaceful acceptance. "It is only by way of our inferior function that the heavenly element can enter. There is no other way."[4] Only in this way can we experience that which we have never allowed ourselves to experience before. "Listen through your heart," Miller told the class, "and you will understand what you have not understood before."

In the hatha yoga science of mind and body it is said that we must stand on our heads to receive this kind of wisdom. Thus our heads will be closer to the earth, pressed against it, and the soles of our feet will reach into heaven. Whatever concepts or cherished beliefs we have held as sacrosanct will be turned up side down. Only then will we see the other side of the issue in this act of sacred prostration.

Johnson claims that the concepts of sacrificial goat versus sacrificial lamb must come together. It is a question of rational and irrational thoughts making friends. My feeling function had to begin by loving my thinking function. My irrational joy, when black women appear in my dreams, as I watch them walk down dusty roads, is partially explained. Here are the scapegoats freed from their oppression. Here is my own soul freed from its dark burden and lightened by this image. Joy and acceptance, I realize, are closely allied. We do not need to sacrifice our sexuality or our worthiness. We are not naturally filled with sin or insane urges for orgies. What is required of us is to acknowledge our inner and higher goodness and to accept the responsibility to do our inner work. And it is work. I once asked Swami Radha the point of spiritual practice. This, she explained, was the work. And the rewards for this daily and often arduous practice would be insights, awareness, and being prepared for the cherished state of self-realization that one could only hope for in this lifetime.

Sacrifice and humility are related to light and projection, and light has been on my mind since infancy. Again I remember the dust motes that carried light to my crib. What do sacrifice and humility have to do with the awe I remember as a child whose first toy was light? My mind has never known how to pray. Instead I sit at the dinner table, put my hands over the food on my plate and imagine light as it repairs indifference in the preparation of our dinner. I block out negative comments I have heard about the contributions of aubergine to arthritis or tomatoes or peppers for that matter. I say to the food, "I'm sorry I treated you so offhandedly. I'm glad you're here. Thanks." In this simple acknowledgement is prayer.

Rather than scapegoating and pointing fingers at those whose sexuality, rage or sense of worthiness is out of control, we would benefit by acknowledging the mother of God as the author of our lives. The little things, done on a daily basis with the attitude of offering and as spiritual practices in their own right, would give our actions and their intentions a quality of purpose and integrity. Brother Lawrence describes what it means:

> I possess God as tranquility in the bustle of my kitchen . . .
> as if I were on my knees before the Blessed Sacrament . . .
> It is not necessary to have great things to do. I turn my
> omelet in the pan for the love of God . . . When I cannot do
> anything else it is enough for me to have lifted a straw from
> the earth for the love of God.[5]

This quote reads like a prayer. It is the perfect way to begin the archetypal journey toward the feminine, the goddess, toward devotion to Divine Mother who is the mother of God. Small actions become holy rituals and bring an importance to our days. They fulfill our spiritual needs. It is the difference between impoverishment and enrichment. It is not our neighbor's goods or wife or money that makes a person rich; it is the loving touch to every moment, the care in every action. Swami Padmananda, a devotee of Swami Radha, once instructed me to begin this daily practice by placing symbols as reminders in each room of my home. I chose to put depictions of Divine Mother in her many manifestations that had meaning to me. They are reminders to me each day of my purpose.

As the mother of God, she is the mother of all gods as well as spouse to them all. This is written in early Vedic texts such as the *Kurma Purana*. "She is said to live in the mouth or mouths of Brahma."[6] She is always on the tip of his tongue. So closely are these gods and goddesses related that they are sometimes referred to in their androgynous form as locked in an embrace. The implication, of course, is that the cultivation of our love for this mother of God is synonymous ultimately with our connection to God, as well. After all, an insult to one's mother is an insult to one's father, too. Daughter, wife, mother: how do we begin to restore honor and respect to her manifestations? We have been in exile too long.

10

Divine Mother:
Redemption and Renewal
Swans I Have Known

There are swans I have known
but very few. Most swans
seek solitude from the fray
in the middle of a lake . . .

> *alone.*

for the sake of poetry
they have been known to swim
for days to clear their bodies
then gaze at the sky . . .

> *throats open.*[1]

If we are very lucky an archetype appears to us, whether in a dream or in our waking life. Mine appeared in daylight on a fishing stream in the Scottish Highlands. It was a mother swan swimming arduously upstream with her cygnets on her back. She held her wings in a raised position from her shoulders so they would all be sheltered from the rapids and the rushing water currents. She was protecting her little ones with every ounce of her strength. She was magnificent, numinous and aglow in the sunshine, there on the radiance of life's stream that swirled around her and rushed by. I had no idea at the time what an archetype was, nor was I aware of the effect of its numinous and holy quality within my own psyche. But that is how it felt. That is what I experienced. It was as if the image of that swan took on even greater significance as the years went by.

One of the things that first touched me in western Canada, where we moved not long after I had seen that mother swan, was a place called Lac des Arcs. There, early each spring, a vast flock of great trumpeter swans lands to rest and feed on its way back to the Arctic.

In his essay "He Who Hunted Birds in His Father's Village: The Dimensions of a Haida Myth", Gary Snyder delves into the significance of the oral Swan Maiden myth, its many versions and possible sources, as a fragile reminder of the swan's poetic existence. Why has it survived across cultures and mythic territories? For what purpose and in what mysterious ways is it a subject that interests literary anthropologists or ethnologists or dream analysts? The swan, accepted messenger bird between the gods and humans, is also about exile from and adoption of other cultures. We have all been exiles and wanderers in our ancient and collective memories, and the swan myth reminds us of this fact. In the Haida myth a man reaches beyond his limits when he tries to marry a swan maiden. He can never hold on to this bird, which is a messenger of the Creator. The longer he tries to hold on to her the more pronounced are his struggles.

The symbol of the swan is about the power of beauty and love to help us in the transformation of attitudes. It is about the help of such a messenger to transcend the limitations of knowledge. Snyder points out that an interpretation of a myth from the outside of any given culture is impossible, for we see into the structure and mythic story our own concerns and insights. This is the power of myth: the empowerment of those who hear and respect its motifs. Nevertheless, my attraction to swan myths has enabled me to identify certain aspects of the swan archetype that pertain to my own reality. Here and there, as I am attracted and drawn closer to swans, their essential characteristics have spoken to my psyche at different times in my life and in varied circumstances in which I have found myself. From fiercely protective mother to poet, to reflective later years, my fascination with swans has always been instructive and often inspirational.

In 1980, during my first visit to the sanctuary of Yasodhara ashram, I took a ten-day "overview of yoga" class. In a workshop called the Life Seal each of us was asked to do a collage, depicting symbols of our positive and negative traits, each of our five senses and last, but most important to me, our essence. A beautiful swan came to me, gliding across a reflective pond. I was enchanted. I recognized her to be my essence.

I discovered, eventually, that she is also my power animal.

What I did not understand was the reaction of the swamis in the room that day at the ashram, when I explained my own life seal. At lunchtime I was handed a note from Swami Radha, asking me to come for a visit to her home that afternoon. She greeted me cordially at the front entrance, led me into the living room and served coffee and cookies. When the conversation got down to the purpose of this unusual visit, I was asked about my swan essence. We talked all afternoon, for I discovered that this was Swami Radha's symbol of essence, as well. The swan is also the blessed messenger of the goddess Saraswati to whose order Swami Radha belonged. Saraswati is the goddess of great knowledge, especially in regard to poetry, music and beauty.

The poetry and beauty did not surprise me because the year after I discovered Lac des Arcs, I took some poetry classes at the university. The poetry of W. B. Yeats and the "Swans of Coole" swam in my head in all the awesome beauty that Yeats could convey. The holiness of swans and their grace had entered my soul. I never spoke of them to anyone, but that year I began to write poetry. That same year my beautiful swan daughter was born. I watched over her and protected her, loved and cherished her, like a swan mother.

What came to my mind at that time was the fairy tale "The Ugly Duckling", about the duck that was really a swan. I remembered with great clarity how that same story affected me so poignantly as a child. Perhaps the image of the swan had been with me longer than I had realized.

The ugly duckling version of the swan is certainly different from the valiant mother swan, struggling against the current. My own mother had been so different from the numinous mother swan. She was more like the duck mother who raises an ugly duckling in an awkward and strange manner while doting on her real little ducks. Seen from the perspective of an adult, I find it hard to blame her. Instead, I have come to understand her.

The Idea of the Holy written by Rudolph Otto is about the awakening of awe. The other worldly aspect of the archetype is, of course, irrational and unexplainable, as it is our only means of connection to the divine. In a literal sense the archetype is the winged bird messenger between the earth and the heavens. It is also the archetype in an image filled with light. To get too close to it all at once is to risk conflation or being swallowed by the Great Mother, she who is beyond our grasp. This is why Forrest Gump catches a glimpse of a feather falling to earth. Though he is innocent and simple, even Gump is not allowed to see the holy messenger who is in touch with God directly. This gently falling feather mesmerizes us.

So, too, we are attracted by the wings of angels and by the dove, which symbolizes the holy spirit. This holy bird is also a messenger and brings good tidings, especially during the happiness of the Christmas season.

In First Nations council meetings sometimes a feather is given to someone who has been a good spirit for the benefit of the community. An entire headdress of feathers is indicative of great service. As such, the experience of the holy "cannot, strictly speaking, be taught, it can only be evoked and awakened in the mind; as everything that comes 'of the spirit' must be awakened."[2]

In its mode of awakening there are as many examples as there are individuals. The awakening may be gentle and slow or ecstatic and wild; it may be reverent and awe-inspiring or purely creative in its urge to manifest beauty and intensity. Regardless of the form of awakening, it is always cocooned in a mysterious and heart-arousing depth. Sometimes it is accompanied by a fear of God as the heart stops and the breath catches.

Because what the image connects us to is unimaginable, we stand in wonder, with a plea that this wondrous happening will not disappear. In these few moments of caught breath we will never forget from whence we come. There will never again be any doubt of where we will return beyond our present existence. This is the numinous realm of the archetype that resides in the unconscious, the realm of the Great Mother. She is the great Brahma of creation, the Black Madonna, the poetry delivered on the back of the messenger swan. It is she unto whom a child is born.

Whether it is Christ who is also black like his mother or an earth born child or a child of creation born to our psyche, all of these symbols stand for redemption, renewal and transformation. What is newborn is possibility in the world. The time of aimlessly wandering is in the past and the soul is united with its higher self.

Jung describes this alchemical process in his *Mysterium Coniunctionis*, as the first stage in which guilt dissolves in the union of bride and groom or the union of consciousness with the unconscious. Between them, as each takes on the attributes of the other, is reconciliation and nourishment. Black guilt takes on the soft beauty of the beloved. Beyond blackness, she glides across the quiet water with power and strength, able to move in and out of the unconscious to attain psychic and spiritual healing.

Jung refers to this process of making-whole as individuation. In the kundalini yoga system it is call self-realization. The effort to become conscious puts us on a path unlike anything we have yet to encounter. It cannot be taught or described because it will be different for each of us. One of my favorite Catholic sages, Teilhard de Chardin, describes it this way:

> The man fell prostrate to the ground. A great silence fell around him . . . a confused feeling that the force which had swept down upon him was equivocal, turbid, the combined essence of all evil and all goodness . . .
>
> Son of man, bathe yourself in the ocean of matter; plunge into it where it is deepest and most violent; struggle in its

currents and drink of its waters. For it cradled you long ago
in your preconscious existence; and it is that ocean that will
raise you up to God."[3]

There may be no one who has said it better than Teillard de Chardin,
the sainted poet, philosopher and wanderer among the peoples of the East
who brought East and West together.

In my last semester at the Jung Institute I was invited to a workshop
in the Glaronese Alps with instructor Edith Sullwold. There were ten of
us in a small chalet and creativity was the theme. When I saw the clay that
was available for use, I naturally began to sculpt a swan. That was the first
day. The next day I met a non-workshop person in the communal dining
room. She was a musician, so I asked her if she knew much about Poulenc.
"Oh, yes," she offered, "He was a great devotee of the Black Madonna."
I was stunned. What had come to me in the concert at Paradaplaz were
Poulenc's devotion and his adoration of the Madonna through his oboe
concerto. I went back to the workshop session bemused.

Immediately after our lunch break I was asked to tell the group about
my sculpted swan. One part of my story was about Swami Radha who
had died that year. I told the group of her swan essence and of my sadness.
Edith listened intently as I spoke. Tears of grief and healing followed. Then
Edith told the group she understood my devotion as she had also known
Swami Radha quite well and had loved her. Edith Sullwold died not too
long afterward. I consider that day a blessing, one of many synchronistic
events overseen by the messenger swan and the Black Madonna.

Saraswati's familiar companion was always the swan; music, poetry,
beauty and wisdom filled the air. The swan, itself called *hamsa* in Sanskrit,
refers to the sound of the breath. It is a natural mantra that changes from
hamsa to *so'ham* as we inhale and exhale. It is one of the most important
mantras attributed to Brahma, said to have both masculine and feminine
aspects.[4] In its cosmic effect it is similar to the sound of OM or AMEN.

Just as in the process of individuation, whereby the individual defines
his or her own personality as distinct from that of the collective, the swan

flies with the exhilaration of freedom. In my case, the swan takes flight to bring back from the universe occasional and unexpected healing and glimpses of transcendence that fill my world.

Introversion and extroversion come together in the healing and uniting of opposites within. Less extroversion and more deliberate attempts at interior reflection have changed my perceptions. I made this an important part of my meditation practice. These days, though I know I am a feeling type, I have cultivated my second function, which is intuition. My sensate function, which lies in my shadow, has been robbed of some of its shadowy qualities. As my introversion is practiced, I notice that bodywork is more appealing to me than it once was. My fight with my computer, while ongoing and fear-filled, has produced some lovely photo projects, emails and information that have proven useful. As for my inferior thinking function, occasionally I remember to listen from my heart. That always works. Listening and making inquiries of my heart helps me to go beyond misunderstanding and outward form. It is the part of my meditation practice that takes me farther than any other activity along this path.

Silence is associated with the swan. Beyond the discipline of meditation, silence is a state of being. Through silence we discover our authentic identity. Infinite balance is also referred to as bliss and is the opposite of speech. When we are renewed through silence we see our speech and daily actions differently. In silence we find strength, ecstasy and stillness. I imagine a swan as it glides across the water of emotion, and a sacred silence descends while I sit and wait.

The goal after all, is the state of individuation or wholeness. In Western Christianity we keep ourselves focused on the difficulty, even impossibility, of this task. In the East this is not so impossible a task and is undertaken by hermits and monastics, householders and those who give of themselves in acts of selfless service. The state of mind individuation or self-realization becomes a process. In a cooperative union between the unconscious and consciousness, we gradually come in touch with the higher good of the universe and our sacrifices are deliberate and focused. Laws become inner states. Messengers, like the holy ghost, may arrive disguised as swans, directing us to our participation in this process of self-realization. Thus, my path and yours will not be the same. Not even our best friend can tell us what to do to achieve this state. Each one must gather facts and examine motives. It takes great effort to stay on this path toward union or wholeness. Conflicts can be overcome and Divine Mother helps in this process when intention is sincere. We call this help grace. In the early church priests and prophets undertook this process in secret. Later it was the alchemists who took up the task, again in secret. They came to understand that "the divine world-soul could be liberated from imprisonment in matter."[5] Their search for spiritual gold was a metaphor for enlightenment. For those who mistakenly searched for real gold the second prize went to the chemists of the future.

In her work with asanas in *The Hidden Language of Yoga* Swami Sivananda Radha explored this hidden gold found in the insights released by the body during the practice of hatha yoga. For years I was afraid of this practice. Whereas most Westerners begin their study of yoga through hatha yoga exercises, I was wary of the disappointment and the limitations that had been my lot in childhood. I simply did not have the courage to confront demons and restrictions. My rebellious front was just that, a front. Somehow I knew that all my failures and shames were hidden there, where I had put them and where I continued to punish myself for these weaknesses, as I saw them. There was to be no forgiveness for the eight-year-old who did not succeed in playing the violin or the ten-year-old who could not pay for dance classes or the fifteen-year-old who had no access to music lessons. There would be no second chances for the young artist who could not stand up for her artist muse and there would be no words for the writer of dark thoughts.

Last year, on a shamanic journey, I encountered some of these young voices. They were crying to be heard. I saw a vision of my many thwarted efforts to write in stacks of paper locked in dark closets. I became the words on those pieces of paper. I discovered myself there, locked in the darkness. Then came the realization that my words and my self were one and the same and that I was being cruel by imprisoning them in the dark. I returned home to write, tentatively at first, in a photo journal of a pilgrimage to Tibet. Now I explore my relationship with Divine Mother. It feels like a journey beneath my skin where there are aches and pains associated with the unlocking of doors. Some issues blink out at me, exposed for the first time in years to gentleness and a welcoming acceptance. There are others I have forgotten about so I have begun a slow search of boxes in the basement. I do not want to become overwhelmed because there is a lot there. If I open them too fast, I could end up piling these thoughts in other corners and never getting to them. Needless to say, these demons are actually daemons, and they fill my heart with their willingness and their lack of spite. How could they await their release all these years without a desire for revenge? I marvel at their love of me, their long-time jailer. This is forgiveness, I realize, true acceptance and kindness. They have waited so long for me to uncover them. I think of the days and hours at Einsiedeln waiting, waiting in front of the Madonna or listening to her water spring, a constant reminder of the flow of grace never-ending. She is my beloved who has never stopped loving me. This inner child whom she watches over is also divine, beloved, me and my inner self. When the Black Madonna approached me in a vision during a Poulenc concerto to say, "Look what we do to the children," I understood, yet I chose to misunderstand. Of course, the children of the world have been subjected to many atrocities over time. Wars have as their victims the young and the old, the beautiful and the good. However, I hear more in that statement today. All these little people inside of me who were victims were the children within who were being shown to me. Barely born, still in a swaddling cloth, they were bleeding and injured, and they were child aspects of my own personality that had never been allowed to grow. I weep for them and for myself. Then I pick up each one, look at the scrunched up little faces and smile. "You're going to be okay," I tell them one by one.

I dreamed of a newborn recently, born to one of my First Nations clients. Before he was born, his mother's dream of him was prophetic. While his parents untangled themselves and came to terms with where he would be registered and raised, he cried and I held him. "You're going to be okay," I told him. "Divine Mother is surely watching over you." I knew the dream was about my own newborn child aspects and the many treasures they will uncover.

It is no mere coincidence that the Truth and Reconciliation movement commenced in the summer of 2010 in Winnipeg, Manitoba. The First Nations people whose stories were being told were there to let their small child, abused personalities out into the light. Many were afraid to let them out, knowing how hurt and angry those children were. But I suspect that this process will be a discovery of those real children. They, too, are divine, and they will be released at last to play beside their eighty-year-old captors. Their captors will find amazingly loving and accepting personalities being released. It cannot be otherwise, considering their divine origins.

These origins, which we can perceive only in the form of an archetype of wholeness, are gifts of the Creator. Whether seen in dreams or gliding over a Scottish stream, the archetype expresses characteristics of the deity. The archetype leads us backward and forward simultaneously to our origins and to our future. It is as though we are part of a great circle or continuum from whence we come and to where we will go. Our source and our destination are synonymous. The only difference, it would seem, is what we will carry with us. To punish mistakenly the little child, who is already being denied gifts from Divine Mother, with shame and humiliation for not keeping the gifts safe, is a double travesty of divine justice.

Recently a seven-year-old child was sent to me. I knew I would see him only once, but he had threatened to kill himself. It turned out that his drugged father had thrown him against a wall and shouted, "Die, you little bastard." So now this beautiful boy felt that he was supposed to die. After all, his father certainly did not want him, and his mother had not protected him. I had to begin by explaining that not only was his father sick but that he, the boy, was not the cause of his father's misery. Then I had to tell him he would need to grow up without parents. He loved school and his teachers, so I told him to get as much out of school as it had to offer. His parents had little to offer beyond a bed and some food on the table. I told him the Creator loved him and so did I. He was smart and very loveable. He walked out standing straighter, with his head up. He now lives with his grandmother who denies there was ever a problem.

Children can stand to hear profound truths. It helps them to survive. It is no small thing to be returned to the protection of Divine Mother. I understand. I often wonder if Divine Mother kept hidden for so many years the insights that I slowly and gradually accumulated in order for me to deal with them at my own pace. In the meantime I did my work and lived my life as best I could. I believe that grace accompanies our prayers and the hours of silent waiting and our willingness to trust that we will know what to do next. Grace can be brought to us on the wings of a mother swan.

The process of individuation involves a dive into the unconscious and a flight into consciousness. Its ultimate goal is to unite the two in a metaphorical marriage. This is not a smooth process. It is fraught with particular dangers that include getting stuck in either one of those states or becoming so defensive and fearful that the personality splits apart in order to escape its fears. Schizophrenia and the kundalini experience look quite similar. If the kundalini experience is misused, the danger of staying trapped in either of those states is seriously possible. In my own experience, because that is the only one I can vouch for, my only protection has been Divine Mother. To her do I offer up my prayers and requests for her guidance. There is no substitute for putting the self in her loving hands. Waiting in great trust and the certainty that she will listen and will guide me has been my own form of worship. Once I have received guidance I offer up my gratitude, great gulps and tears of it. There has been no other way for me.

Carl Jung refers to this method of realization as being too difficult for many people. To step onto this path one must step whole-heartedly or become totally neurotic and cut off from the world. Jung claims that failure at this process might cause people falsely to call themselves artists or poets, as if art had nothing to do with ability. "But if you have nothing at all to create, then perhaps you create yourself."[6] Jung was somewhat elitist in this regard, for this statement exposes his view of art and artists that is not necessarily accepted universally. The kundalini system, on the other hand, expects just this act of self-creation to accompany self-realization. Everyone is invited to try to reunite with Shakti, as she tries to unite with Siva. From my first breath I have never been able to choose between masculine and feminine, mother and father. I have practiced drawing circles and I have embraced my own watery nature. It is my own tricky path.

The alchemists referred to Mercurius as the "world-soul imprisoned in matter" . . . who "set free and redeemed." His truth must "be known by meditation, or by *cognitatio*, reflection."[7] Mercury is a kind of slow-moving, watery matter. In the act of reflection one looks within the circle, that is, into the center which contains the experience of all of us, whether that of mother, father, siblings, friends or, from the edge of the circle where there are no sides to be taken. From the center there is only the all seeing, all hearing, free of opposites, even those of masculine and feminine. The circle is inclusive, a spot of light in the darkness that flows through matter. Like Mercury it has no boundaries.

Since early childhood I have been confused as to which side of my body was masculine and which side feminine. A gentle father, a cold mother, a grandmother who was accepting and solid, another grandmother who was weak and sickly but kind; none of it added up. When I did the hidden language hatha yoga my body would speak quite loudly from unexpected sides and places. Then there were echoes, like the voice of wisdom that comes from the land.

Teilhard de Chardin expressed this natural wisdom in his uncanny voyage through the landscapes of the East. China, Mongolia, caravans and steppes, echoed in a collective upwelling of nature and patience derived from the endless cycles of renewal and destruction. They are inescapable. His prayers included the entire universe and his experiences dwelled in the joy and pain of his travels. He was an earth wanderer whose narrative resonates with my own psyche. I, too, had become a wanderer in order to compensate for deprivation. I looked on my travels as a voyeur, expecting to learn from the successes and mistakes of everyone I encountered. Reading his commentaries was worth every second. My eventual conclusion was that I had acquired all I had needed, despite my impoverished beginnings or maybe because of them. We have all come to this place, when we have realized that the past is a part of us, part of our foundation and that it makes us uniquely our own person. No one else has done it or been through it in quite the same way.

One day I cried, feeling overburdened with a certain sorrow that I knew was stuck in my body and I could feel the sorrow flowing out of my body with the tears. When there is a tension of opposites, the tears collect and become stagnant in my body. When the tension is released something else happens.

If the soul gets stuck in the body, the body becomes a prison. In alchemy, Mercurius manifests as a capable healer. But he is capable of just about anything, even evil. He is a trickster. He is a personification of the imprisoned soul. Priests in our era are quite familiar with Mercurius. Celibacy, for instance, instigates the battle that the body fights in order to restore freedom. The outcome of this terrible inner war has many twisted outcomes. Sublimation of the body's desires is not easy and many slip from their good intentions. Once this happens and secrecy or denial find a foothold, evil is given sway. Redemption can only be prayed for and left in the hands of Divine Mother.

In my work with residential school survivors the stories of perversion and cruelty by nuns and priests are endless. As one elder remarked, "These were men of god . . . but I cannot imagine what kind of god it was." Of course, it was god's other half, the devil or his dark side. None of us wants to imagine ourselves pulled into this realm. To be a priest in any age is to suffer identification with the deity. The mass for instance, is a rite whereby the priest takes part in the symbolic transformation of bread and wine into the body and blood of Christ. Day after day priests put themselves in such a dangerous position. Without infinite humility this rite cannot be borne. Shamans and healers suffer greatly as the ills of their people are removed, then dealt with in the body of the shaman. The reason for this suffering is that someone at some point must make the unconscious conscious. It is only then that union is possible, that light penetrates the darkness, that separation, painful separation, is dissolved. "Come," the shaman or the healer whispers, "You are welcome in me. I will be a channel for your pain." In this act there is great trust. In this act there is great love and personal sacrifice. The channel is never to be confused with the source of healing, with God.

At a conference of senior elders of the First Nations in preparation for the first Truth and Reconciliation event in the summer of 2010, I was asked to explain my work with trauma. I looked around the circle after I had explained the newest brain research and my understanding of connecting the two sides of the brain. There were blank and disbelieving stares. This is not going well, I thought. I am not on the same wavelength as these elders.

So I heard myself telling them in story form of my experience with David Miller's seminars in Zurich. By story form I mean all the pauses and embellishments and emphases and personal inserts about my own state of mind as I went through this process of coming to terms with the fact that Miller and I were different personality types. As I watched faces, I saw no more boredom or disinterest. Everyone was understanding or at least engaged in the story. When I finished, there was an important question from one of the elders. "How does one listen through the heart?"

"Practice," I answered, "lots of practice. It does not happen overnight, normally." I referred to the Dalai Lama and his hours of daily meditation. No matter where he travels or how tired he is, he does his practice. Since everyone loves the Dalai Lama, there were nods of acceptance from the group. It all made sense. There are no quick solutions, and this, too, the elders understood.

A decade or so after meeting Swami Radha I decided to do the Life Seal workshop a second time. I was conflicted in my marriage, stood at a crossroad, and wished I could take an easier path, maybe join the residents at the ashram. It was a thought parallel to the one I had had at age thirteen when I had wished to escape to a convent. Oh, how our issues appear over and over again until they are resolved. I felt dried up spiritually and wondered where the swan had gone. Truly, it felt like it had flown away, never to return. However, when we were asked to draw our essence, to my surprise, two swans appeared, facing each other, the shapes of their long necks combining to form a heart shape between them. Since my marriage felt dried out just like my spirit, I felt awe at the irrational appearance of the heart. O Divine Mother, I had so much to learn. My biggest realization that day was the certainty that the dark always awaits the light. Later, I would recognize this dual swan symbol in the heart chakra. Masculine and feminine people who cannot understand each other any other way must come to an understanding through the heart. These form the inner ear of subtle and gentle sounds that can be heard in peaceful reflection. Swans glide across a pond in silence. Their beauty surpasses understanding. They are filled with a grace that is deliberate in motion, humble and vulnerable in a soft curve.

I recite a prayer to Divine Mother that Swami Radha once loved. It comes from the *Ananda Lahari: The Blissful Wave*:

> O Divine Mother,
> May all my speech and idle talk be mantra,
> All actions of my hands be mudra
> All eating and drinking be the offering of oblations unto thee,
> All lying down prostrations before Thee.
> May all my pleasures be as dedicating my entire self unto Thee.
> May everything I do be taken as Thy worship.

This prayer hangs in my office just behind the right shoulder of my clients where they sit during analysis. It reminds me that everything I say or hear or understand comes through Divine Mother first. It is her manifestation that causes the words. I try to listen carefully. Then, in the times I do not understand what is going on, I bring in the statue of the Black Madonna that I bought in Einsiedeln. She is hand-carved of a hard wood and beautifully smooth and unassuming. I sit her there on a table between us and wait. Inevitably, that day my client is her client. He or she ends up pouring out problems for Divine Mother to sort through. It is as though I am not there and she listens, she intervenes and she shows great compassion and understanding. Today, my intention is to bring her in, as a young couple tries to deal with a new baby, as they decide to go their separate ways or not. Perhaps Divine Mother will look beyond their opposite and seemingly insurmountable problems to come up with a third idea, a solution.

Two swans, the heart, the Madonna, the mothers I have known, the mandala of the heart as inscribed on the earth and in water is witnessed in heaven. I feel such gratitude to all my teachers: my own mother, all the surrogate mothers, Swami Radha, and Carl Jung, who never gave up trying to understand his feminine side. I whisper my thanks: to the Black Madonna who sought me out and gave me her great blessings I kneel in gratitude; to my higher self who was nurtured by my father and his mother, who believed in Christ's saying that forgiving seven times seven, over and over, was the key to the heart. All these years and efforts I hope will carry me through. Forgiving the small child, being loving to those little ones inside, seeing those little ones in others, recognizing the little ones who still need to be carried beneath a swan's wings until they can paddle upstream on their own: all are ongoing commitments to my self. O Divine Mother, how beautiful is this life, its tears and sorrows, its joys and insights, its bliss whenever I feel your feathers brush along my spine or sing out in a poem of witness and praise.

ENDNOTES

CHAPTER 1: *MOTHER ARCHETYPE, BIRTH TRAUMA, REBIRTH*

1. Aurobindo, *The Mother,*
2. Keats, *Ode to Psyche,* line 43.
3. Rank, *The Trauma of Birth,* 114.
4. Plato, *Phaedo,* 77.
5. Rank, *The Trauma of Birth,* 114-5.
6. Ibid., 115.
7. Ibid., 123-4.
8. Neumann, *The Great Mother,* 136.
9. Ibid., 137
10. Waley, *The Way and Its Power,* xxiv.

CHAPTER 2: *THE GRANDMOTHERS: GRANDMA, SHAMANS, THE GIFT OF THE PRISM*

1. Campbell, *Myths of Light,* 132.
2. Bear Heart, *The Wind is My Mother,* 56.
3. Shakespeare, *Love's Labour's Lost,* I, i, 237.
4. Briffault, *The Mothers,* 15.
5. Ibid., 275.
6. Jung, *Collected Works: Volume Nine, Part One,* 69.
7. Ibid., 157.
8. Ibid., 102.
9. Jung, *Collected Works: Volume Seventeen,* 9.
10. Waley, *The Way and Its Power,* xxv.
11. Neumann, *The Origins and History of Consciousness,* 31.
12. *Taittiriya Upanashad* 2.2.

13. Harding, *The Parental Image,* 105.Storm, *Seven Arrows,* 10.
14. Jung, *Collected Works: Volume Seventeen,* 292.
15. Tedlock, *The Woman in the Shaman's Body,* 67.

CHAPTER 3: *MOTHER SURROGATES, SYMBOLS*

1. Goethe, *Faust,* 175-6.
    a. Rider, 52.
2. Jung, *Collected Works: Volume Six,* 153.
3. Jung, *Collected Works: Volume Six,* 172
4. Jung, *Collected Works: Volume Fourteen,* 667.
5. Jung, *Collected Works: Volume Nine, Part One,* 161.
6. Thomas, *"Fernhill",* poem #130.
7. Jung, *Collected Works: Volume Five,* 449.
8. Radha, *The Hidden Language of Hatha Yoga,* 34.
9. Jung, *Collected Works: Volume Twelve,* 438.
10. Ibid., 439.
11. Nietzsche, *Ecce Homo,* 179.
12. Jung, *Collected Works: Volume Fifteen,* 128.

CHAPTER 4: *OTHER MOTHERS: CHURCHES, CRUCIBLES, RITUALS AND WHOLENESS*

1. Jung, *Collected Works: Volume Five,* 313.
2. von Bingen, 30.
3. Jung, *Collected Works: Volume Eleven,* 778.
4. Ibid., 778.
5. Ibid., 75.
6. Woolf, *Moments of Being,* 40.
7. Jung, *Nietzsche's Zarathustra: Volume One,* 692.
8. Walker (Ed.), *The Woman's Encyclopedia of Myths and Secrets,* 1077.
9. Jung, *Collected Works: Volume Six,* 377.
10. Ibid., 803.
11. Ibid., 804.

CHAPTER 5: *MOTHER NATURE: ENERGY, EVIL, EXPERIENCE*

1. Norberg-Hodge, *Ancient Futures*, 157.
2. Schopenhauer, *On the Suffering of the World*, 3.
3. Eliade, *Yoga: Immortality and Freedom*, 202.
4. Feuerstein, *Yoga: The Technology of Ecstasy*, 258.
5. Eliade, *Yoga: Immortality and Freedom*, xvii.
6. Hauer, *Yoga as a Path to Heaven*, 58. In Jung. *Kundalini Yoga.*
7. Yeats, "a terrible beauty," 17.
8. Goethe, *Faust*, 21.
9. Rumi, 30.

CHAPTER 6: *NEGATIVE MOTHERS: THE DARK SIDE OF MOTHER*

1. Bachofen, *Selected Writings*, Refer to chapter on Lycia.
2. Plato, *Republic* 9, 575.
3. Jung, *Collected Works: Volume One*, 12-13.
4. Jung, *Collected Works: Volume Five*, 570.
5. Jung, *Collected Works: Volume Eleven*, 157.
6. Jung, *The Undiscovered Self: The Dilemma of the Individual in Society*, 83.
7. Neumann, *The Great Mother*, 148.
8. Jung, *Collected Works: Volume Ninne, Part One*, 168.
9. Jung, *Collected Works: Volume Thirteen*, 55.
10. Jung, *Collected Works: Volume Eighteen*, 74.
11. Perera, *The Scapegoat Complex*, 91.

CHAPTER 7: *MOTHER OF DREAMS*

1. Freud, *Dream Interpretation*, 97.
2. Jung, *Collected Works: Volume Eighteen*, 523.
3. Ibid., 482.
4. Ibid., 500.
5. Radha, *The Divine Light Invocation, 2.*
6. Norbu, *Dream Yoga and the Practice of Natural Light*, 46.
7. von Franz, *On Dreams and Death*, 147-8.
8. Hollister-Wheelright, *The Death of a Woman*, 22.
9. Ibid., 271.
10. von Franz, *On Dreams and Death*, 150.

11. Meier, *Healing Dream and Ritual,* 112.
12. Ibid., 113.
13. von Franz, *The Way of the Dream,* 214.
14. Plath, *"Daddy",* 17.
15. Jung, *Collected Works: Volume Eighteen,* 250.
16. Asper, *The Inner Child in Dreams,* 5.

CHAPTER 8: *ENDLESS ENERGY: ATTITUDES, EXPECTATIONS; WHERE IS MOTHER?*

1. Jung, *Collected Works: Volume Eight,* 2-3.
2. Campbell, *Occidental Mythology,* 259.
3. Campbell, *Primitive Mythology,* 436.
4. Cooper, *Illustrated Encyclopedia of Traditional Symbols,* 148-50.
5. Irving, *Serpent of Fire: A Modern View of Kundalini,* xx-xxi.
6. Jung, *Collected Works: Volume Five,* 246.
7. Ibid., p. 248.
8. Campbell, *The Inner Reaches of Outer Space,* 89.
9. Greenwell, *Transformations.*
10. Irving, *Serpent of Fire: A Modern View of Kundalini,* 62.
11. Canadian Mental Health Association (www.cmha.calgary.ab.ca)

CHAPTER 9: *MOTHER OF THE DAWN: MADONNA AND TRANSFORMATION*

1. Neumann, *The Great Mother,* 33.
2. Ibid., 336.
3. Ibid., 310.
4. Jung, *Collected Works: Volume Six,* 149.
5. Brother Lawrence
6. Brown, *God as Mother,* 150-151.

CHAPTER 10: *DIVINE MOTHER: REDEMPTION AND RENEWAL, SWANS I HAVE KNOWN*

1. Nemetz, *Caffe Beano Anthology: Volume One,* 24.
2. Otto, *The Idea of the Holy,* 7.
3. de Chardin, *Hymn of the Universe,* 60-65.
4. Feuerstein, *The Deeper Dimensions of Yoga,* 168.
5. Jung, *Collected Works: Volume Eleven,* 448.
6. Ibid., 906.

References

Alighieri, Dante. *The Divine Comedy: Inferno: Volume One.* Translated by Mark Musa. New York: Penguine Books, 1971

Angelou, Maya. *I Know Why the Caged Bird Sings.* New York: Random House, 1969.

Asper, Kathrin. *The Inner Child in Dreams.* Translated by Sharon E. Rooks, Boston: Shambala Publications, Inc., 1992.

Aurobindo, Sri. *The Mother.* Pondicherry, India: Sri Aurobindo Press, 1977.

Bachofen, J. J. *Myth, Religion and Mother Right: Selected Writings.* Translated by Ralph Manheim. Princeton, NJ: Bollingen Series LXXXIV, Princeton University Press, 1967.

Bair, Dierdre. *Anais Nin: A Biography.* New York: Penguin Books, 1996

Barrows, Kate. *Ideas in Psychoanalysis: Envy.* Edited by Ivan Ward. Cambridge, England: Icon Books, Ltd., 2002.

Bear Heart & Molly Larkin. *The Wind Is My Mother: The Life and Teachings of a Native American Shaman.* New York: The Penguin Group 1996.

Bingen, Hildegard. *Hildegard of Bingen's Book of Divine Works: With Litters & Songs.* Edited by Matthew Fox. Santa Fe, NM: Bear & Company, 1987.

Book of Changes. Translated by Richard Wilhelm & Cary F. Baynes. Princeton, NJ: Princeton University press, 1967.

Bosco, Antoinette. *Mother Benedict: Foundress of the Abbey of Regina Laudis: A Memoir.* San Francisco: Ignatius Press, 2007

Briffault, Robert. *The Mothers:A Study of the Origins of Sentiment and Institutions.* NY: Atheneum Press, 1977.

Brown, C. M. *God as Mother: A Feminine Theology in India: An Historical and Theological Guide to the Brahmavaivarta Purana.* Hartford: W. Claude Stark, 1974.

Campbell, Joseph. *Myths of Light: Eastern Metaphors of the Eternal.* Novato, CA: New World Library, 2003.

_____. *The Masks of God:Occidental Mythology* and *Primitive Mythology. Vol.3 & 1.* Novato, CA: New World Library, 1959-1968.

_____. *The Inner Reaches of Outer Space.* NY: Harper and Row, 1988.

Cooper, J. C. (ed.) *Illustrated Encyclopedia of Traditional Symbols.* New York: Thames and Hudson, 1978.

Daly, Mary. *Beyond God the Father: Toward a Philosophy of Women's Liberation.* Boston: Beason Press, 1973

Daly, Mary. *Gyn/Ecology: The Metaethics of Radical Feminism.* Boston: Beacon Press 1978.

Darwin, Charles. *On the Origin of Species.* Edited by David Quammen. New York: Sterling Publishing Co., Inc., 2008.

De Chardin, Teilhard. *Hymn of the Universe.* New York: Harper & Row, 1965.

De Roy, Tui. *Galapagos: Islands Born of Fire.* Falls Church, VA: Charles Darwin Foundation, Inc.

Eckhart, Meister. Edited by Bernard McGinn. New York: Paulist Press, 1986.

Eliade, Mircea. *Yoga: Immortality and Freedom.* Translated by Willard R. Trask. London, England: Arkana, 1989.

Evans-Wentz, W. Y. (ed.) *Tibetan Book of the Dead.* London, England: Oxford University Press, 1960.

Freud, Sigmund. *The Interpretation of Dreams.* Translated by A. A. Brill. New York: The Macmillan Company, 1913.

Galland, China. *Longing for Darkness: Tara and the Black Madonna.* New York: Penguin Putnam Inc., 1990

Goethe, Johann Wolfgang von. *Faust: Part One.* Translated by Philip Wayne. London, England: Penguin Books, 1949.

Greenwell, Bonnie. *Energies of Transformation: A Guide to the Kundalini Process.* Cupertino, CA: Shakti River Press, 1990.

Gustaphson, Fred. *The Black Madonna.* Boston: Sigo Press, 1990.

Harding, M. Esther. *The Parental Image: Its Injury and Reconstruction.* Edited by Daryl Sharp. Toronto: Inner City Book, 2003.

Hillman, John & McLean Margot. *Dream Animals.* San Francisco: Chronicle Books, 1997.

Hollister-Wheelright, J. *The Death of a Woman: How a Life Became Complete.* New York: St. Martin's Press, 1981.

Hurston, Zora Neale. *Dust Tracks on a Road: An Autobiography.* Edited by Robert Hemenway. New York: Harper & Row Publishers, Inc., 1984.

Irving, Darrel. *Serpent of Fire: A Modern View of Kundalini.* York Beach, MA: Samuel Weiser, Inc., 1995.

Johnson, Robert. *Ecstasy: Understanding the Psychology of Joy.* Harper San Francisco, 1987.

Jung, C. G. The Psychology of *Kundalini Yoga: Notes of the Seminar Given in 1932 by C. G. Jung.* Edited by Sonu Shamdasani. Princeton, NJ: Bollingen Series XCIX. Princeton University Press, 1996.

_____. *The Collected Works.* (Bollingen SeriesXX) 20 vols. Translated by R. F. C. Hull. Edited by H. Read, M. Fordham, G. Adler. W. McGuire. Princeton, NJ: Princeton University Press, 1953-1979.

_____. *Flying Saucers: A Modern Myth of Things Seen in the Skies.* Translated by R. F. C. Hull. Princeton, NJ: Princeton University Press, 1978.

_____. *Nietzsche's Zarathustra: Volume One.* Edited by James L. Jarrett. Princeton, NJ: Bollingen Series XCIX. Princeton University Press, 1988.

_____. *The Undiscovered Self: The Dilemma of the Individual in Society.* Translated by R. F. C. Hull. New York: New American Library, 2006

Keats, John. "Ode to Psyche" *The Complete Poems.* Edited by John Barnard. New York: Penguin Books, 1988.

Kiely, R. *Blessed and Beautiful: Picturing the Saints.* New Haven, CT: Yale University Press, 2010.

Lawrence, Brother. *The Practice of the Presence of God.* London, England: The Epworth Press, 1984.

Lincoln, Victoria. *Theresa: A Woman.* Edited by Elias Rivers & Antonio T. de Nicolas. State University of New York Press, 1984.

Meir, C. A. *Healing Dream and Ritual: Ancient Incubation and Modern Psychology.* Daimon Verlag, 1989.

Nietzsche, Friedrich. "Between Birds of Prey" in *Ecce Homo.* Translated by Walter Kaufmann. New York: Vintage Press, 1967.

Nemetz, Virginia. "The Poetry of Swans" in *Caffe Beano Anthology: Volume One.* B House Publications, Calgary, AB, Canada. 2008

Neumann, Erich. *The Origins and History of Consciousness.* Translated y R. F. C. Hull. Princeton, NJ: Princeton University Press. Bollingen Series XLII, 1954.

_____.*The Great Mother.* (Ralph Manheim, Trans) Translated by Ralph Manheim. Princeton, NJ: Princeton University Press. Bollingen Series XLVII, 1991.

Norberg-Hodge, Helena. *Ancient Futures: Lessons from Ladakh for a Globalizing World.* San Francisco, CA: Sierra Club Books, 2009.

Norbu, Namkhai. *Dream Yoga and the Practice of Natural Light.* Edited by Michael Katz. Ithaca, NY: Snow Lions Publication, 1992.

Otto, Rudolf. *The Idea of the Holy.* Translated by John W. Harvey. Oxford, England: Oxford University Press, 1954.

Perera, Sylvia B. *The Scapegoat Complex: Towards a Mythology of Shadow and Guilt.* Toronto: Inner City, 1986.

Plath, Sylvia. *The Collected Poems of Sylvia Plath.* New York: Harper & Row, 1981.

Plato *Phaedo: Collected Dialogues.* Translated by H. Tredennick. Princeton, NJ: Princeton University Press, 1961.

_____. *Republic: Collected Dialogues.* Translated by H. Tredennick. Princeton, NJ: Princeton University Press, 1961.

Rank, Otto. *The Trauma of Birth.* New York: Harper & Row, Publishers, Inc. 1973.

Reik, Theodore. *The Secret Self.* New York: Farrar, Straus & Young, 1952

Rumi, Jelaluddin. *Feeding the Shoulder of the Lion: Selected Poetry & Teaching Stories from the Mathnawi.* Putney, VT: Threshold Books, 1991.

Schaefer, Carol. *Grandmothers Counsel the World: Women Elders Offer Their Vision for our Planet.* Boston: Trumpeter Books, 2006.

Shakespeare, William. *William Shakespeare.* Edited by W. J. Craig. Oxford, England: Oxford University Press, 1930.

Schevill, Margaret E. *Beautiful on the Earth.* Santa Fe, NM: 1947.

Schopenhauer, Arthur. R. J. *On the Suffering of the World.* Translated by Arthur R. Hollingdale. London, England: Penguin Books, 2004.

Shipiro, Francine. *Eye Movement Desensitization and Reprocessing.* New York: The Guilford Press, 2001.

Singer, June. *Boundaries of the Soul: The Practice of Jung's Psychology.* New York: Doubleday Anchor Books, 1989.

Sivananda Radha, Swami. *Hatha Yoga: The Hidden Language: Symbols, Secrets and Metaphors.* Porthill, ID: Timeless Books, 1987.

_____. *The Divine Light Invocation.* Spokane, WA: Timeless Books, 2006.

_____. *Kundalini: Yoga for the West.* Spokane, WA: Timeless Books, 1978.

Sri Sankaracharya. *Ananda Lahari: The Blissful Wave.* Swami Sivananda, Trans. Calcutta: The SP League, 1949.

Storm, Hyemeyohsts. *Seven Arrows.* New York: Ballantine Books, 1972.

Stephenson, Craig E. *Possession: Jung's Comparative Anatomy of the Psyche.* New York: Routledge, 2009.

Snyder, Gary. *He Who Hunted Birds in His Father's Village: The Dimensions of a Haida Myth.* Bolinas, CA: Grey Fox Press, 1979.

Tedlock, Barbara. *The Woman in the Shaman's Body: Reclaiming the Feminne in Religion and Medicine.* New York: Bantam Books, 2006.

Tenzin Wangyal, Rinpoche. *The Tibetan Yoga of Dream and Sleep.* Edited by Mark Dahlby. Ithaca, NY: Snow Lion Publications, 1998.

Thomas, Dylan. *The Poems of Dylan Thomas.* New York: New Directions, 2003. von Franz, Maria-Louise. *On Dreams and Death.* Translated by Emmanuel Xipolitas Kennedy & Vernon Brooks. Boston: Shambhala, 1987.

_____. *The Way of the Dream.* New York: Frazer Boa, Publisher, 1987.

Waley, Arthur. *The Way and Its Power: A Study of the Tao Te Ching and its Place in Chinese Thought.* Cambridge, 1934.

Wolf, Fred Alan. *The Dreaming Universe: A Mind-Expanding Journey into the Realm Where Psyche and Physics Meet.* New York: Simon & Schuster, 1994.

Woolf, Virginia. *Moments of Being: Unpublished Autobiographical Writings.* Edited by Jeanne Schulkind. London, England: Triad Grafton Books, 1981.

The Woman's Encyclopedia of Myths and Secrets. Edited by Barbara G. Walker. San Francisco, CA: Harper & Row, Publishers, 1983.

Yeats, William Butler. *The Collected Poems of W. B. Yeats.* London, England: Wordsworth Poetry Library, 1994.